Making Your O

CHE

Making Your Own
CHEESE

How to make all kinds of cheeses in your own home

PAUL PEACOCK

A HOW TO BOOK

ROBINSON

ROBINSON

First published in Great Britain in 2010 by Spring Hill,
an imprint of Constable & Robinson Ltd

Reprinted in 2015 by Robinson

7 9 10 6

A CIP catalogue record for this book is available from the British Library.

ISBN: 978-1-90586-248-1

Note: The material contained in this book is set out in good faith for general, guidance and
no liability can be accepted for loss or expense incurred as a result of relying in particular
circumstances or statements made in the book. Laws and regulations are complex and liable to
change, and readers should check the current position with relevant authorities before making
personal arrangements.

Designed and typeset by Mousemat Design Ltd
Printed and bound in Great Britain by Ashford Colour Press Ltd, Gosport, Hants

Robinson
An imprint of
Little, Brown Book Group
Carmelite House, 50 Victoria Embankment, London EC4Y 0DZ

An Hachette UK Company
www.hachette.co.uk

www.littlebrown.co.uk

How To Books are published by Robinson, an imprint of Little, Brown Book Group. We
welcome proposals from authors who have first-hand experience of their subjects. Please set
out the aims of your book, its target market and its suggested contents in an email to
howtobooks@littlebrown.co.uk

CONTENTS

CHEESE: THE
MIRACLE FOOD

As a child I used to be sent to the shops for what was then termed 'cooking cheese'. It was a kind of Cheddar: slightly hard, full-fat, strongly flavoured, ideal for melting. It was twenty years before I realised I was eating strong Cheddar. What my mother termed 'eating cheese' was Cheshire, which was crumbly. We never saw Stilton or Danish; you simply couldn't buy those in inner-city Manchester.

Thankfully, the arrival of a supermarket opened a new world of opportunities for cheese. We were suddenly exposed to Roqueforts, ricottas, wonderful Edams and Gruyères. Cheese lost its mystique for us, and while it became more commonplace, at the same time certain types remained grand and desired.

Even today, we still don't really understand cheese. We like flavours and textures – like many wine-drinkers we 'know what we like' – but the step from buying cheese in a supermarket to making your own remains a pretty daunting prospect for most people.

And yet, making cheese is one of those things that, for centuries, humans have done to survive. Its origins stretch right back into the dawn of agriculture. However, it is much more than a mere 'survival tool'. Cheese is one of those foods that make life bearable – and to me, real culture is just that: something that makes life bearable.

Which is why, although this book will show you how to make cheeses in many categories, it has only one theme: that cheese should be enjoyed by everyone.

Indeed, cheese is culture at its best.

How it all began

We can only speculate about the consequences and technology that came together to create cheese. On one hand, most people know that if you leave milk for long enough you get a semi-solid, strongly aromatic mass few of us would actually wish to eat. On the other hand, it is quite a leap to work out that these two portions, solid and liquid, separate and that you can wash away the 'off' portion, leaving behind coagulated protein.

Yet the fact that every culture in the world has a simple, basic cheese made in almost the same way suggests a common ancestry. Even the Chinese, who aren't noted for dairy products, make a simple cheese called *bai*, which is similar to Asian paneer, South American *queso blanco* and so on. It was in Europe, however, that cheese-making developed into the range of delightful culinary treats we know today.

The development of Brie, for example, is a little miracle in itself. Its manufacture depends on exact temperature management and the application of a fungus during the maturation stage. How eighth-century cheese-makers were able to keep milk at the required temperature, when a variation of just one degree can ruin the cheese, is still unknown, yet they were obviously successful at it – so much so that when Holy Roman Emperor Charlemagne first tasted Brie, he asked that the town's taxes be paid not in money, but in cheese.

Whatever its origins, cheese was possibly first mass-produced in Greek times, but the Romans were the true cheese-masters. They preferred smoked cheese, and also invented the cheese press. It wasn't until the fourteenth century that moulds for pressing cheese into specific shapes were invented. In medieval times, monasteries were the major movers in terms of cheese manufacture, and most commonplace cheeses we know today started life in cloistered surroundings. From the Middle Ages onwards, the popularity of cheese exploded exponentially – particularly because most royal families gave it as presents to courtiers at Christmas.

Why make your own cheese?

This book is designed for anyone who wants to make cheese for his or her own use – not sell it to others. The reason for this is because I believe we will one day have to rely on the skills my grandmother had for our everyday existence.

My grandparents lived modest lives in industrial districts, went to work in an effort to keep the country from the grasp of Nazi Germany, and yet still had time to grow and produce much of their food. Cheese was a fundamental part of their world. When they had cheese melted on grilled bacon with a splash of milk to make the sauce, it was their own cheese they used. Forgive me for sounding pessimistic, but their skills, I believe, are the key to mankind's success in future years.

So my answer to the question 'Why make your own cheese?' is based partly on this concept: that the skills and knowledge humanity has used over generations are just as important today as they were a thousand years ago.

Yet there is something more we have missed out on along the way. If you make your own cheese and become proficient at it, you are making a product that is wildly better than anything you could buy in the shops. You know its origin; you know there is nothing in it other than what you put into it; you control its saltiness, additives and flavour. It is *your* cheese – and as such, it is better than any other.

Is it cheaper?
Not if you have to buy the milk, but it can be. It will, however, certainly be cheaper than those posh cheeses you purchase at the shops. You can make a very good Boursin alternative with very little fuss, for example, and it will be *your* cheese.

When is the best time to make cheese at home?
Summer makes for more even temperatures; consequently maintaining milk temperature is easier. But nowadays, the best time to make cheese at home is anytime you fancy cheese!

Types of cheese

Making Your Own Cheese contains recipes for the following cheese types, described here in brief but elaborated on in later chapters. Their successful manufacture depends just as much on your ability to store and mature them as on each recipe's heat treatments and starter requirements.

While ancient cheese-makers relied on microbes from their locality, modern cheese-making uses microbes purchased in a sachet. The difference between a creamy Lancashire and a Stilton is due to the starter and microbes used in the process, but centuries ago it resulted simply because there were different microbes in the environment where Stilton was made than were present in Lancashire. Microbes aside, however, all cheeses can be divided into the groups listed below.

Fresh
Fresh cheese is the simplest type to make. Milk is soured, either with rennet or sometimes with lemon juice, and the resulting whey is allowed to drain away naturally. The mass, or curd, is simply collected in a cheesecloth and washed to remove as much of the whey as possible, then salted. Sometimes cream is added, but otherwise this is all that's involved in the process.

Soft cheese
Soft cheeses are made by the action of a starter inoculation and rennet. When the cheese has been made, it is then washed in a fungal solution to achieve its final form. Camembert and Brie are familiar examples of soft cheeses.

Veined cheese
Veined cheeses are hard or crumbly cheeses that have been inoculated during the maturing process with either special fungi or bacteria. They have blue or sometimes green or green/yellow veins which are formed wherever the bacteria or fungi have come into contact with air. Stilton and Gorgonzola are good examples of veined cheeses.

Hard cheese

Hard cheeses are pressed. While pressing doesn't create the hardness as such, it does extract the final amounts of whey from the cheese. The consistency and flavour of hard cheese comes from the starter, which is added to the milk at the beginning of the cheese-making process.

Cooked cheese

Cooked cheese is a hard cheese that has been cooked. Emmental is one example: its texture has been changed by being cooked for around an hour. Cooked cheeses are often painted with wax.

Goats cheese

Goats milk cheeses are white cheeses created by the fat globules present in goats milk, which are much smaller than those found in cows milk. Generally soft, goats cheese can sometimes be hard and more acidic in nature than the more familiar cows milk cheese.

Ewes cheese

Sheeps milk produces both soft and hard types of cheese, and both are usually strongly flavoured and creamy. Pecorino, for example, is a little like Parmesan, while Broccio is a very creamy soft cheese that is similar to ricotta.

Smoked cheese

There are various smoked cheeses, some of them processed and inexpensive, others full-bodied and crafted. Most cheese-makers consider apple wood as the best wood for smoking cheese, but other types can be used, depending on personal taste.

Processed cheese

Many cheese spreads and slices are more industrial than the specialist craft cheeses that make up the focus of this book. What we think of as American cheese, for example, was developed to cover hamburgers, and is made by blending various cheeses, then cooling them in strips.

HOW CHEESE IS MADE

One thing I'm asked more than anything else is 'How do you make cheese?' For some reason, people believe it is one of the most difficult things in the world, while in fact it is quite simple.

Milk: the main ingredient

Obviously, cheese is made from milk. The milk of any domesticated farm animal can be used to make cheese: cow, goat, sheep, buffalo, reindeer … even yak. The methods of making cheese may vary, but no matter which animal it comes from, it all starts with milk.

Milk is a miracle food. It contains essential nutrients for infants, be they calves or lambs, human babies or newborn yaks. Some of these nutrients, such as sugar, are 'water-soluble' – they dissolve in water. For example, milk contains lactose, a milk sugar, that is essentially dissolved in water. Yet some nutrients, including many proteins and vitamins, are fat-soluble, and these are also contained in milk, dissolved in fat globules in suspension within its watery portion. This fat not only provides an infant with important fat-soluble material needed for growth, it is also a source of energy.

Every mammal on earth owes its life to milk. It has all the nourishment needed to sustain life, grow an immune system and bones, and it provides the energy needed for life to develop further.

Why milk spoils

Bacteria in milk feed on milk sugars, which are found in milk's 'watery portion'. As they feed, the bacteria excrete an acid called lactic acid. When the pH of the liquid reaches 4.2, milk protein, known as casein, coagulates and you end up with a smelly, yucky mess. The milk spoils, or 'smells off', and we discard it.

Yet this isn't the whole story. Bacteria only consume the sugar that is present in milk; they leave its protein and fat portions untouched. Separating the 'off' portion from the rest is what gives us the perfectly good, edible product known as cheese, and to do this under controlled circumstances, you must curdle the milk to make it separate.

There are a number of ways of doing this, but the two most common are by directly adding acid and using an enzyme.

Using acid

In Africa it has long been usual practice to drink the paunch liquid of certain antelopes as a strategy for avoiding dehydration. Of course, this liquid is acidic, but it is mainly water and thus suitable for drinking, because the antelope used this liquid as 'storage' in case of drought. Yet it is still acidic enough to curdle milk, so it may well be that 'antelope acid' was used to make the world's first cheese.

As mentioned earlier, every culture has a basic cheese, based on the addition of acid, be it in the form of lemon juice or vinegar. During typical simple cheese-making, milk is heated to quite high temperatures and then the acid is added. The whey is discarded and the remaining curds are washed until they are no longer acidic. This type of cheese is often cooked again, then preserved in brine or oil.

Rennet

Rennet is the curdled milk found in calves' stomachs (although vegetarian rennet is also available these days). It has often been said that the enzyme route to creating cheese was discovered when people first cut open a calf's stomach to find this clotted material inside.

Personally, I find this a difficult proposal, but we do know that Egyptians, and probably the Mesopotamians and Persians, used to dry animals' stomachs to use them as containers for liquids. These vessels could easily have leached a substance that did in fact clot milk. Because these 'stomach bags' date from around 4000 BC, this really is remarkable.

How cheese gets its flavour

A good cheese gets its flavour in two ways. Firstly, the creamier the milk, the better the flavour (well, that's my opinion, at least). Cheese made from a 'factory' milk cow, a poor genetically 'enhanced' animal that makes five gallons of milk a day, is never going to taste as good as that made from milk from a Jersey that produces barely one and a half gallons of really thick, creamy milk. The fat content of milk is an important part of any cheese.

The second flavour aspect comes from bacteria present in the cheese. Some, such as lactobacillus and listeria, originate in milk; others are found in the environment, and still others, such as lactococcus, are added.

There are mainly two types of bacteria that are added to cheese: mesophillic, which can withstand temperatures up to around 30–40°C; and thermophillic, which can withstand even hotter temperatures. In a nutshell, mesophillic starters make softer cheeses, while thermophillic starters make harder, more robust cheeses – although, as we shall see later, this isn't always the case.

Flavour in cheese can also come from different types of fungi, which are usually added at the maturation stage. Brie, Roquefort and Camembert, for instance, are all made with a penicillium fungal wash. In some cases the fungal wash creates a white crust and the cheese is soft and dissolved. In other cases, fungi react with oxygen to create a number of different colours: anything from grey or green through to blue.

APPRECIATING CHEESE

Whenever two people come together there will be two differing opinions about cheese. Thankfully, though, the language that surrounds cheese-making is generally exempt from the kind of nonsense adjectives used to describe fine wine (especially wine from France). But in a way, real cheese, the type made in farmhouses by small farmers or at home, or made by craftsmen according to recipes that are hundreds, if not thousands, of years old, has a provenance and *terroir* in the same way as fine wine. And this means that the 'making' of cheese, and its appreciation, is affected by more than straightforward ingredients.

The *terroir* aspect

Cheese varies according to where its made – from farm to farm, from pasture to pasture. It is often all too easy to forget that cheese is simply nature's processed grass, and as such is subject to the vagaries of the weather, the soil, the fertility of the land – i.e. the *terroir,* in wine terms – as well as the genetics of the animal that produced the milk and, of course, the skill of the cheese-maker who produces it.

To enter into the making of cheese, whether you are a dairy farmer, a small goat herdsman or an enthusiast in your own home using bought milk, is to join a long line of miracle workers that stretches back to the beginning of civilisation.

Cheese should certainly be enjoyed. It is not just a staple, like potatoes, to be fed to the masses, but even where it does take on such a role it is almost worshipped. The difference between a pecorino and a Parmesan might seem small to some, but it means all the world to Italian mothers feeding hungry families.

The English, by contrast, have long thought of cheese as a separate part of a meal, often to be served only at the end in the form of a cheese board. But around the world cheese is and has traditionally been a fundamental part of any main meal.

Wine and cheese

If you remember wine-and-cheese parties, you will be of a certain age. They were all the rage in the 1970s and usually consisted of Cheddar on sticks with apple or pineapple and some very dubious wine. The French, however, take wine and cheese very seriously and believe the two flavours complement each other. Although we in the UK take the combinations of cheese and wine with a pinch of salt (not literally), there is certainly something in what the French say.

As a general rule of thumb, light red wines are best served with soft cheeses: Beaujolais and Brie make a classic combination. Stronger, more robust wines are needed to accompany blue-veined cheeses, which themselves have a stronger flavour. The extra saltiness of blue cheese matches deep red wine, such as Bordeaux, very classically.

Of course, the UK has its own traditional cheese dish that can only be best enjoyed with a pint of good beer. In my opinion, the ploughman's lunch cannot and should not be eaten with anything else!

Cheese and crackers

Crackers were the 'fast food' of Victorian times, and the best, to my mind, are small, thin and made from rye. The original idea behind the cracker was to add another texture to a meal; according to etiquette, they should not be dramatically larger than the tiny morsel some people load on them. In France they still debate at length, even after many hundreds of years, whether you should put butter on your cracker. Well, that's up to you! Personally I prefer unsalted butter simply because this does not detract from the saltiness of the cheese.

Crackers are really only a British and French way of eating cheese. Italians cook their cheese almost without exception, or eat it with soft bread. The rest of the world sees cheese as something to cook, apart from the Americans, who either put cheese on everything, and take a large part of it from a cellophane wrapper or worse still, a tube. To be honest, there are a number of good farmhouse cheeses in America, but when you visit, you frequently only see the processed cheeses.

Cheese by season

Like all agricultural processes, there is an element of seasonality to cheese. The UK is among the best places to grow good-quality grass, and this is reflected in the quality of our cheeses.

The best cheeses in the world come from wherever grass grows best. Northern Europe has mountainous valleys where the temperature and rainfall make for good grass. There, grass starts to grow in April and stops in October. During the winter months, when cattle are stalled and fed on hay, silage or pellets, there is a perceptible difference in the quality of cheese made from their milk.

Since cheese is frequently left to mature, it is possible to 'release' it for sale over a period of time, and, generally speaking, the following cheeses are available and good all the year round. We are talking here about bought cheeses from specialist suppliers and cheese shops, but homemade cheese can be made very successfully at any time of the year.

Summer cheeses
Blue farmhouse cheeses • Most goats-milk cheese • Ewes-milk cheese

All of these are better between May and October. Later than October and they have been refrigerated a little or are a little on the ripe side.

Winter cheeses
Brie • Camembert • Stilton • Mature cheeses such as strong Cheddar

Nearly all UK cheeses are fine all year round, as are very hard cheeses such as Parmesan, and northern European cheeses.

Storing and serving cheese

Bought or made, cheese is best stored in cool temperatures. You should not put cheeses in the coldest part of the refrigerator, but at a reasonable distance away from it, so that they never really chill, but are kept in a condition where they can continue to mature.

Soft cheeses particularly need time to mature properly. If you were rich enough to waste a few soft cheeses (dreadful thought!), on slicing through them you would find an ever-decreasing ring of maturity. This is why you should try to avoid eating a soft cheese until it has been rested for a few days (but if you're anything like me, you will find resistance difficult).

You can store cheeses in an airtight container, partly to keep the moisture in, partly to save the whole fridge from smelling like it. A single droplet of water on a tissue in the container will create the perfect conditions for cheese maturity.

Before serving, give cheese a chance to breathe. Leave it to come to room temperature and never allow it to be warmed (or cooled for that matter) too quickly. Only serve small quantities at any one time. Continual warming and cooling of cheeses increases the possibility of bad bacteria – which is why you should avoid returning pieces of cheese to the refrigerator from the cheese board. They will invariably have been handled and contaminated and who knows what will grow on them? It's best – and more enjoyable – to eat them up there and then.

MILK, STARTERS AND OTHER INGREDIENTS

There was a scientist, whose name I cannot remember, who believed that milk must be intrinsically sterile. His reasoning was that once the milk was left to stand in the kitchen it would go off in a very few hours, but it was always fresh inside the cow's udder. In experiment after experiment he found that milk started to go off as soon as it was taken from the cow; therefore, he reasoned, the environment inside the udder must be absolutely sterile.

The truth is that a cow's udder is far from sterile; indeed, it is full of bacteria. If the cow were to die, the milk would go sour inside her udder. The fact of the matter is that bacterial growth is carefully controlled by a cow's udder – and bacteria are a vital part of milk's overall food value.

What does milk contain?

For a mammal, milk is one of the most complete foods there is. It is made up mostly of water, but its 12% of solids range from fat, vitamins and enzymes to hormones, sugars and minerals. Milk really is a miracle food, providing all kinds of benefits. It is crucial to the development of mammals, and the entire class of animals depends on it completely. No milk: no mammals.

Milk sugars
Milk sugars are made from a simple carbon molecular ring known as a saccharide. The majority of these sugars consists of lactose, but there

are others. Lactose is a disaccharide, which means it has two molecular rings stuck together. The chemistry needed to create this molecule occurs in the milk-secreting cells of an animal's udder. Lactose is easily broken down into other sugars: glucose, fructose and galactose.

It is thought the developing brain of any mammal needs these various sugars in order to grow. Other milk sugars play a role in supporting a healthy immune system, fighting some pathogens and promoting healthy bacteria in the gut. So milk sugars are wonderful things in themselves – and they are vital to making cheese, although they are rarely mentioned by cheese-makers or cheese-making books.

Yet the fact is that microbes in milk rarely respire, or breathe, in the same way as other living organisms. They are not very efficient at breaking the bonds in lactose to release the simple sugars they need. For most organisms, sugar is metabolised using oxygen, and the end result is carbon dioxide, water and energy. Most microbes present in milk need no oxygen, but instead of releasing carbon dioxide, they excrete lactic acid.

It is this acid which, building up in the cheese, eventually causes the protein portion of milk to clot. Yet milk has 'gone off' well before its acidity has reached pH 4.2 – the necessary clotting point – which is why it smells and is usually discarded. Leave it alone, however, and it will clot and smell even stronger. This is usually enough to put anyone off the idea of trying to make their own cheese, yet like all magical processes, the result of cheese-making is nothing like these smelly dregs.

Protein

As mentioned previously, milk contains a number of different proteins that are necessary for various functions in young mammals. We also use two of these proteins in cheese-making. The first is casein, which is more or less a 'lego kit' of amino acids, easily broken down and reconstituted by young mammals. Moreover, casein is the molecule that clots when acidity increases. When it clots, it traps fats and sugars inside a globule, and it is this that is ultimately pressed to make cheese.

The second protein used in cheese-making is albumin, found in the watery portion of milk and simply washed away with the whey in many cases. However, albumin will precipitate when whey is boiled, and this is used to make ricotta.

Some ricotta recipes call for large quantities of whey; others produce an acceptable alternative cheese made from a combination of casein and albumin. Ewes milk has a much higher concentration of albumin than cows milk, which is why it is particularly good for making ricotta.

Goats milk is slightly lower in protein and consequently a little harder to set than cows milk. Ewes milk is significantly higher in protein and consequently is much prized for cheese production.

The nature of the curds depends on the type of milk used. Cows milk gives a 'sticky' or more robust curd which is easy to handle – which is why this is probably the best milk to use when making your first cheese. You can handle the curd without really having to worry about it falling to pieces.

Goats and ewes milk both make softer curds, which can have a tendency to break up and become a slurry. You need to handle these more carefully, and while it is clearly not impossible to get it right the first time, you're probably best using cows milk when you start out.

Fats

Fat molecules in milk are very high-energy storage bodies, but they have many functions other than simply providing long-term energy. Many proteins are soluble in fat rather than water, and they have important roles to play in the production of a good immune system. Because the whole of our sensory and nervous systems depends on fats, you can imagine how important they are to a young animal.

Milk contains both saturated and unsaturated fats. Whole milk is about 3.3% fat, two-thirds of which are saturated. For the cheese-maker, fat means flavour. Of course, you can make cheese from skimmed milk and get a product which is lower in fat, but it won't have that much flavour. However, you could add other flavours, such as garlic or chives, to increase its appeal.

Minerals

Generally these are of nutritional value but don't add much in the way of flavour. Probably the most useful mineral for cheese-making is calcium. The absence of calcium promotes weak, floppy curds.

Colour, creaminess and flavour

Milk is not always white; its colour runs the gamut from blue-white through creamy white to snow-coloured. Milk's colour usually depends on two aspects: the quantity and size of the fat molecules, and whether the animal has been passing carotene into the milk.

Goats don't pass on carotene and their milk contains much smaller fat globules., which is why it is much whiter than cows milk. Ewes milk, which is very white, is similar, but its fat content is higher than either goats or cows milk, and the resulting cheese can be slightly coloured.

Generally speaking, the creamier the milk, the better flavour the cheese has. Consequently, not all cheeses are the same because they come from different animals. Over the border from our home lives the biggest herd of Jersey cows in Europe, and the cheese made from these beautifully wide-eyed ladies is marvellous. If you make cheese from one of those automaton cows whose pitiful existence yields five or more gallons of milk a day, then your end result will reflect this.

A note for smallholders

It's possible to make perfectly good cheese from bottled milk bought at the supermarket. I do it all the time. But, like me, there are many who dream of their own little patch of land and a house cow (or goat) from which to make dairy products. If you're going to make your own cheese from your own animals, there are a number of things you need to remember, and the first involves milking.

I'm not going to teach you how to milk; this is a skill best learned from a mentor. But you must maintain absolute cleanliness when milking your animals in order to avoid contamination. Wash their udders with udder wash, cleaning them as much as possible, then milk a little into a separate cup and examine it. Look for blood and clots in the milk, which could be signs of a bacterial infection called mastitis.

Milk carefully into a sterilised bucket; from here the milk needs to be filtered and cooled. Filtering is easily done through a fine mesh, which also needs to be sterile. Cooling is also important because the bacteria inside are doubling in number every 20 minutes.

Pasteurisation

It is illegal to sell unpasteurised milk or milk products in several countries, and there are a number of excellent reasons for treating your milk in this way. While there are many, very vocal, opponents to pasteurisation, I firmly believe you should use pasteurised milk simply because many harmful bacteria are killed during the pasteurisation process.

There are different pasteurisation methods, and when you get into cheese-making you will find that temperature is all-important. For cheese-making you should heat and maintain the temperature to 65°C for 30 minutes. The milk needs to be stirred to prevent it from forming a film. You can do this in a double boiler or a large pan. Some recipes for pasteurisation use higher temperatures, but I have found that these are sometimes detrimental to the final cheeses.

Hundreds of independent cheese-makers swear by unpasteurised milk. They say their cheeses would not be the same without it – and they are probably right. But it is one thing for a small, semi-industrial cottage industry to make cheeses to strict regulations and standards of safety, and quite another for a home producer to use unpasteurised milk safely.

Because this book is foremost for the home cheese producer, we have no scruples in encouraging everyone to make cheese with pasteurised milk. Pasteurisation made it possible for milk to be transported much further, allowing dairy farms to be located out of town, sending their wares to outlying settlements. This simple process has contributed to the spread of mankind almost as much as it has benefited our health.

How milk reacts

Milk responds to changing environments. The many enzymes hidden inside fat globules are released when the fat is broken down. Shaking milk or forcing it rapidly through pipes can release these enzymes, starting the process of digestion and changing the nature of the milk. To get consistent results, always treat your milk with careful respect and treat it the same way every time you make cheese. Routine, cleanliness, temperature control and love make the best cheeses.

It is possible to freeze milk. Goats milk freezes best, then cows milk and then ewes milk. This relates to the rate of denaturisation of fat in the frozen milk. Yet even though it is a viable process, try to avoid using frozen milk if you can use fresh. And remember: just because the milk has been frozen doesn't mean it should not be pasteurised.

Reheating frozen milk should be done slowly. First, simply stand it at room temperature until the milk becomes liquid. Do not try to force this process by standing it in hot water or putting it into the oven; this only accelerates the growth of bacteria and the milk will not last as long as it should.

Powdered milk

Goats milk is sometimes low in protein, so powdered milk is added during the cheese-making process. Lots of people around the world make cheese from powdered milk, particularly in remote areas of the USA and Canada. Usually, cheese from powdered milk is improved by the addition of some cream. Adding powdered milk to goats milk is standard practice for many cheese-makers. More than one company makes a mozzarella cheese using a combination of non-fat powdered milk with added cream. Where necessary, any recipes in this book will call for powdered milk and give tips on where to buy it. It is best to get the very highest-quality powdered milk you can find, however; this is one time the discount brands simply do not work well enough.

RENNET AND WATER QUALITY

While milk is obviously the most important element, a surprising number of additives and ingredients are involved in making cheese. One of the most important is rennet.

Rennet

Before the turn of the first millennium, cheeses were made in stomachs of calves no older than two days. The animals were slaughtered and their stomachs were cut out, emptied and cleaned, then filled with milk which then ripened as a cheese. It was the enzyme known as rennet that was responsible for the curdling.

Rennet allows the curdling of cheese at a lower acidity level than would occur naturally, thus yielding a product that is not so sharp to the taste. For a long time rennet was a by-product of calves – usually unwanted male calves; consequently, vegetarians find it difficult to use comfortably and have for years looked at other ways of curdling milk. There has long been a vegetarian option made from the common plant called lady's bedstraw, but the juice from the plant was never long-lasting and it was difficult to get batches that had a uniform action.

Combinations of lady's bedstraw and nettles were also used, and some European cheeses are still made using thistles as a coagulant.

These days vegetarian rennet is made from genetically modified bacteria which have had a rennet-making gene inserted into them. It is also now possible to get vegetarian rennet that is consistent and strong in action. Certain suppliers call this product chymosin, but it is also known as rennin.

Whether from animals or vegetarian sources, the action of rennet on milk separates the solid portion (curds) from the liquid portion (whey). Actually rennet is a complex mixture of enzymes – chiefly rennin and pepsin.

On average, you only need one drop of rennet to every litre of milk. Four and a half litres – roughly one gallon will require four or

maybe five drops. Using 4.5 litres of milk will yield a decent block of cheese: around 300g.

Chlorinated and fluorinated water

Chloride ions reduce the efficiency of rennet, which is the main reason why you have a good batch one day and a poor one the next: the amounts of chlorine in water vary from day to day. You can remove most of the chlorine from water by boiling it, although you must let it cool thoroughly before using it to dilute your rennet. Alternatively, you can use spring or bottled water, which does not have any chlorine added to it.

Fluorine has the same effect, only more so, and if you live in an area where these chemicals are added to your water, use pure water instead whenever you make cheese.

Storing rennet

Rennet is destroyed by both extreme cold and heat, so keep it in the refrigerator but do not freeze it. It is also destroyed by light, and should be stored in a dark place. For this reason, you'll find that it often comes in light-proof bottles.

STARTERS AND OTHER INGREDIENTS

Starters have a number of functions: increasing the acidity of milk, improving the flavour and creaminess of the cheese made from it, and also influencing the cheese's final texture. The addition of the starter is a ripening process because it continues to work in the cheese right up until the point at which it is eaten – unless of course the cheese is cooked beforehand.

You can buy starters from cheese-making suppliers. They are basically milk powder with bacteria added, which is the reason they create lactic acid and increase the acidity of the cheese. This, combined with the enzyme rennet, clots the milk to form curds, which ultimately become cheese.

Types of starters

Starters can be divided into two types. First there are mesophillic starters. These are starters whose bacteria will not survive high temperatures such as those over 40°C. They are used for making soft cheeses as well as yoghurt.

The second type are known as thermophillic starters. These can withstand temperatures up to around 50°C and are used for making hard cheeses and ones which, like Cheddar, undergo exposure to an elevated temperature for a prolonged period.

However, you can use all kinds of starters when making simple cheese. Plain yoghurt is good, for example, as is crème fraîche, or even single cream. Experiment with varying quantities of these starters and you will soon find a recipe you like.

The starter is fundamentally a bacterial additive, not a dairy additive, although natural ones such as yoghurt obviously combine the two. The fact that cheese can appear creamier because of a starter has more to do with the latter's action than its flavour.

Cheese producers once made their own starters, traditionally from a culture of whey that had been allowed to ferment. The

29

bacteria in the milk were used as the 'inoculation' for the next day's cheese. The 'mother culture' would be used, diluted in whey, but frequently it had to be replaced due to the growth of undesirable bacteria.

These days, thankfully, freeze-dried starters can be used, and are recommended for the home cheese-maker. Dissolve just a couple of grams of starter in a little milk, then leave it to work at room temperature – and that's it. These starters make sophisticated home cheese-making possible because they are easy, exact, highly effective and safe. You don't introduce any stray bacteria when using them, and they also store well.

Salt

It is important to salt homemade cheese because it draws more whey out of the curds, preserves the cheese, stops its continued acidification and, of course, improves its flavour. Ordinary kitchen salt is fine for a number of cheeses, particularly soft cheeses that need little ripening. Most supermarket salt is iodised, however, and these ions can slow down the action of starter bacteria. Actually, chloride ions in salt do the same, but only to a lesser degree. If you are making any cheeses that need to stand, use either special cheese salt, purchased from cheese-making suppliers, or else salt that has not been iodised.

Calcium chloride

Whenever milk is overheated and brought to the boil, some of its calcium content can be used up in the scum or skin that is formed. If cheese is low in calcium it does not set as well as it should. Most home cheese-producers do not have to use calcium chloride, but if you are making goat's cheese, it is possibly a good idea if to do so if you find that your milk never produces good curds

Microbes

Like its main constituent milk, cheese is very much a living product, and as previously mentioned, a number of microbes are used in its production. These are usually added during the final or maturation stages, and the most common are listed below.

Penicillium candidum

The word *candidum* means 'white' in botanical Latin, and this is a white mould. It is usually added as a wash or spray to make Brie. It comes as a powder, which is then diluted and washed over the outside of the cheese. You'll have noticed the *penicillium* part: yes, just like the tablets we get from the doctor, this mould inhibits the growth of bad bacteria in the cheese. However, eating cheeses made in this way will not, sadly, clear up any infections!

It is thought that *Penicillium candidum* was originally added by accident in a cave or cellar, and people soon noticed how much smoother and less acidic the resulting cheese became after treatment. Whatever the truth about its origins, its use in cheese-making goes back around 1,500 years.

Penicillium camemberti

Similar to *Penicillium candidum*, *Penicillium camemberti* is a white mould that is not so popular among home cheese-makers, except when making goats cheese. It has a similar action to *candidum*, but is, if anything, more aggressive.

Penicillium roqueforti

If you know your cheese, you will instantly realise that this is the mould used when making blue cheeses. In addition to changing both the flavour and structure of the cheese, *Penicillium roqueforti* reacts with oxygen to create blue colours, and, contrary to popular misconception, it provides a cheese that is almost free from harmful bacteria because the blue stains actually repel them. This is one cheese that is certainly not 'off' in any way!

CHEESE-MAKING EQUIPMENT

We have already looked at the very basic ingredients you need in order to make cheese; now it's time to consider the implements you need to use. The process is generally a simple affair, but it can sometimes seem complex if you're trying to make more exotic cheeses. I must say that I prefer to make simple cheese; it is useful and easy, and if you're making cottage cheese, then the most basic pieces of kit are all you'll ever need. Yet from time to time I do like the challenge of making more complicated traditional cheeses – the kind you would buy in the shops. Whatever type you choose to make, though, you'll need the same basic equipment to get you started.

The good news is that most cheese-making is easy, and if you have a decently stocked kitchen, then you should already have the bulk of what you need.

ESSENTIAL EQUIPMENT: THE MINIMUM

Pans

You need a pan that can hold and heat 4.5 litres (approximately one gallon) of milk. The milk must be heated accurately to within one degree, and sometimes this is best done in a purpose-made double boiler or by putting a pan in a water bath.

Finding a double boiler that holds a gallon is no mean feat, but try to find a good, deep pan with straight sides so that your thermometer can stay on well (see below). Even then, you'll need to practise with your cooker for a few times until you are able to reach and maintain a constant temperature.

Thermometer

To do the above successfully, you must have a very good thermometer that is easy to read. Never use a thermometer as a stirrer; you will invariably break it and could injure yourself; you will certainly spoil your cheese.

There are a number of different thermometers on the market these days, with dials and pointers that are fine so long as you can see them well enough to within one degree. If not, however, then simply use a standard heatproof glass one. Jam thermometers are fine as long as you

can read specific temperatures, but be aware that you need a range of at least 20–50°C. You will need to heat milk to 80°C if you are making paneer; otherwise, most cheeses are heated to between 25–35°C, with a few other exceptions.

A good cheese thermometer has a lip that allows you to keep it in place on the side of your pan. Before using, always sterilise your thermometer; it may look clean, but this doesn't mean that it actually *is* clean.

Skimmer

A skimmer is a ladle with lots of holes in it that is used for getting curds out of whey. It is especially good for making goats cheese because you don't want to wobble the curds about too much.

Curd knife

You probably have a knife big enough for getting down to the bottom of the pan when making cheese. Some recipes call for the curds to be cut into cubes, which are then cooked to reduce their size; you then remove some of the whey from them. The curd knife can be a pallet knife or anything long enough, really, but one with a flat end is a great help.

Cheesecloth and muslin

Cheesecloth and muslin are used to drain whey from the curds, as well as lining moulds prior to pressing. You pour the cheese into a muslin-lined colander (usually a double layer), pull the corners together and then hang it to drip-dry.

Although the two can be used interchangeably at times, there is a difference between cheesecloth and muslin. Cheesecloth has a larger weave, but to be honest, it is just as good for the purpose because you use a double thickness of it in any case.

However, there are different grades of cheesecloth. The everyday, cheapest type is not that well-made; it loses strands (which no one likes in their cheese) and will not withstand boiling. For this reason, always buy cheese-making-grade cheesecloth: it's easier to use and is more robust, and can cope with being boiled.

Make sure your sheets are around 50cm square; this makes them big enough to tie up and hang. Unless you're going to collect your whey to feed to the pets or to make ricotta (but you need quite a lot to achieve this), the best place to hang a dripping cheese is from the tap over the sink – or from a washing line (which is how my grandmother used to do it).

Cheese moulds

These are plastic and usually round. In fact, most moulds are plastic these days, easily cleaned and sterilised with boiling water. Be sure to get all the cheese out of the holes every time you clean the mould. There are many sizes available, but for the home producer the smallest is fine.

Although it does shape the finished product, basically, a cheese mould is used to get more whey out of the cheese. Since whey contains sugar, its presence in cheese will quickly cause it to spoil. Frequently whey is washed out of the cheese, leaving watery curds, and you want to get as much of this water out of your cheese as possible. Dripping does work, but the application of pressure as a secondary procedure is also used.

To press a cheese, line the mould with cheesecloth and, once the curds are in place, put the 'follower' (or plunger) on the top and apply pressure to it. Simple heavy weights can be used for this purpose, or you can use a special cheese press (see page 38). Even for very hard cheeses, pressing rarely occurs for longer than 12 hours, and the home cheese-maker really only needs one or two moulds at most.

Cheese presses

The old-fashioned wooden Dutch press, shown below, is a great piece of equipment and it is also easy to make at home. But actually you don't need it, as an old 'G' clamp will suffice just as well. Over the years I have seen many different kinds of contraptions used for pressing cheese – bungees have been the most recent. They work well, but you have to be careful when releasing the pressure.

Perhaps the most useful cheese press is one of those universal steel presses (below). They can be used for cheese, fruit and even pressed meat, are easy to clean, and are one of the most versatile utensils in the kitchen.

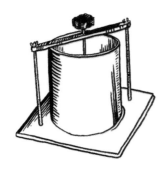

Hygrometer

A hygrometer is used to measure humidity. If you are going to make cheeses that ripen over a period of time, you need a reliable way to measure humidity. Too humid and you run the risk of the cheese becoming mouldy and inedible.

Wax and wax brush

Cheeses such as Edam (and many more besides) are matured in wax. This is usually brushed on as an easy-peel food-grade wax that is available from cheese-supply companies. You can use any good-quality brush so long as it has natural bristles and not plastic ones; the latter tend to melt into the wax if it is very hot.

Caring for your equipment

It is very important that your equipment is kept completely clean at all times, which involves not only sterilising it, but physically cleaning every piece of kit. Deposits of dried-on cheese can be difficult to remove, but you should work at it until it is completely clean.

Where possible, buy easy-to-clean, high-grade plastic equipment. Not only is it less likely to collect debris and is easy to clean when it does, but it is cheap to replace when you can't.

The other good thing about plastic is that it is not troubled by acidity during the cheese-making process. The colour might fade a little, but it won't introduce or leak any taints or spurious chemicals into the mix.

BASIC CHEESE-MAKING

Cheese, like oil, makes too much of itself. It wants the whole boat to itself. It goes through the hamper, and gives a cheesy flavour to everything else there. You can't tell whether you are eating apple pie or German sausage or strawberries and cream. It all seems cheese. There is too much odour about cheese.

Jerome K. Jerome

In this book we're not concerned with descriptions of 'copyrighted cheeses'. We are here only for the home consumption and enjoyment, so we can make ourselves a 'Camembert' or a 'Roquefort' and then enjoy our efforts without selling it and stepping on anyone else's 'patent'.

While I spoke briefly of cheese types on pages 9–11, this chapter goes into them in more depth before showing you how to make your first simple soft cheese. This is so that you know exactly what types of cheeses you can produce in your own home – and they are all based, more or less, on this first simple cheese. The descriptions may seem a little confusing because the terms 'soft' and 'hard' are used, but they are only comparative. Even the hardest cheese is not that hard, really; you couldn't knock a nail in wood using a pecorino or a Parmesan, for instance!

The descriptions on the following pages also transcend nationality. Some people tend to list cheeses as 'Italian' or 'French'; still others like to list them by milk type as 'cows' or 'goats', but I think a description of the actual cheese itself is best.

TYPES OF CHEESE

Soft cheese

Cheeses that are unripened or not pressed are described as soft. Cottage cheese, for example is a soft cheese. Some would say it was a 'runny cheese', or a 'wet cheese', but whatever you call it, a true soft cheese should never be pressed.

That said, you can press cottage cheese if you wish; just gather up the curds and force all the liquid out and it will harden quite easily.

Ripe cheese

These are soft or semi-hard cheeses that have been 'fermented' (not in the alcoholic sense, though!) by the action of a fungus or bacterium (or both) to produce a homogeneous softness. Brie is just such a cheese which is inoculated with a penicillin-type fungus during its final stages of production. The result is a rich, creamy, often runny cheese.

Semi-hard cheese

These cheeses are probably best described as 'crumbly'. They are lightly pressed, but the structure still crumbles as you cut it. Creamy Lancashire belongs in this group, as does Caerphilly. Cheshire can be crumbly; depending on who makes it, it is sometimes a little harder.

Semi-hard cheeses are ideal for the home producer because they do not need so much pressure in production; therefore less equipment is necessary. You can make a small cheese very easily by using a few weights on the follower of your cheese.

Hard cheese

The term 'hard cheese' is British in origin and refers to how disappointing it is to discover cheese that has dried up and become hard. Yet hard cheeses such as Cheddar simply refer to the fact that cheese has been subjected to large pressures. These cheeses are made using various production techniques, then the last drops of whey are forced out of the cheese before ripening. Their texture is altered to produce a uniform, cheesy mass which is left to mature before use.

Cooked cheeses

There are a number of cheeses where the curds are cooked before they are moulded and ripened. This forces liquid out of the curds in the cooking, altering the curds' nature. Sometimes the cheese is cooked and then rolled or sheeted, as in what we call 'American cheese', and a large number of tubed or creamed cheeses are cooked.

Blue and inoculated cheeses

All cheeses are inoculated in one way or another, sometimes accidentally. However, a whole series of the most popular cheeses in the world are purposely infected with fungi at the ripening stage. One group contains the soft, runny cheeses such as Brie, while others are given fungi that react with oxygen to create a blue or green, white or grey colour.

The reason for doing this is not just because it makes the cheese 'pretty'. The fungus also 'digests' the cheese, creating quite a different flavour. Blue cheeses have an interesting combination of flavours and increased acidity, as well as frequently increased creaminess. Some take on subtle, musty tones, too, from time to time. The flavours also develop with age, as does the smell.

MAKING YOUR FIRST CHEESE

Possibly the most important thing to get across about cheese-making is cleanliness. Implements, cheesecloth, containers, draining boards … everything must be sterile. It is important not to introduce stray microbes into your cheese, because you're going to leave it to mature and don't want spoiled cheese or poisoned guests.

The following recipe is for a simple cheese that really works very well. You can use this cheese as the basis for a number of other recipes, and you can make several simple variations from it by adding various extras such as chives, garlic, salt and pepper, fruit or other herbs. It can also be made into a semi-hard one quite easily.

Simple Kitchen Cheese

If using your own starter in this or any other recipe, always use fresh – never stuff that has been in the fridge for any length of time – to ensure that you're not introducing unknown microbes into your cheese. This cheese will last for around five days if kept in the refrigerator.

3 litres pasteurised milk
10ml mesophillic starter
3 drops rennet
1g (¼) teaspoon salt

1. Heat the milk to 30°C and keep it at this temperature for 30 minutes.

2. Add your starter and stir it in well.

3. Leave it for 45 minutes for the acidity to build up and the bacteria in the starter to improve. Just keep your milk in a covered pan (the one you warmed it in will do) and it will more or less keep it's temperature while the starter develops.

4. Boil then cool some water and add 3 drops of rennet to a tablespoon of the water. (Rennet is destroyed at 40°C, and you should never let it get anywhere near this temperature.) Stir this in to the milk, replace the lid and leave it to set for around 30–90 minutes. Don't be tempted to add more rennet; there are many reasons why milk may take a long time to set. Temperatures, the type of rennet, the acidity of the milk all have a role to play, so try to be patient.

5. Once the cheese has set, pour the liquid away as carefully as you can, ladle the curds into a muslin-lined colander, then simply draw the corners together to hang the cheese for 24 hours to drain. You should be left with moist curds.

6. Add the salt, sprinkled evenly, and leave to drain again (salt draws more whey from the curds).

7. Place in a sterile bowl and check the seasoning, adjusting it if necessary. You can add cream or herbs of many kinds, or simply enjoy your first cheese 'neat'.

Mrs Forbes' Cream Cheese

I haven't a clue who Mrs Forbes was, but this is an old recipe and makes another good simple introduction to cheese-making.

Full-fat milk
Salt

1. Fill a pan with full-fat milk and leave it for several days until the cream separates, then hardens. The milk below the cream should be quite thick and beginning to go off.

2. Carefully skim off the cream and place it into a muslin square, drawing the corners together so that it can be hung. As it drips, this cream should become thicker, eventually leaving cheese behind. It should stop dripping after about 3 days.

3. Carefully salt the cheese to taste and place it into a second muslin square, folding the corners over.

4. Place between two boards, pop a weight on top for 24 hours and you will then have cream cheese. Simple!

Whole Milk Cheese

*This simple cheese was made in cottages for hundreds of years. Before salting you could wash the remaining curds out with fresh, gently running water.
This will yield a less pungent cheese.*

Full-fat milk
Salt

1. Start with milk in a pan, as for Mrs Forbes' Cream Cheese (opposite). Allow the milk to go off, then plop the whole lot into the muslin: cream, milk and all.

2. Leave it to hang until it stops dripping, then salt to taste.

HARD CHEESES

No matter how many times you make cheese, it is always different. There are too many variables to control each time, especially when you're alone in the kitchen.

Small producers also have variations in their cheese: sometimes the milk isn't the same, sometimes the starter is weaker, or stronger. When they make new batches of starter there is often a difference in the cheese – not that we would particularly notice, but it's there. Large cheese producers go to great expense to ensure their cheese is the same from plastic-wrapped sheet to plastic-wrapped sheet.

All you can aspire to is that you will keep everything – all the processes, the rennet, the starter, the quantities and temperatures – the same every time you make a particular cheese. On the whole, you're probably going to make only a few cheeses regularly. If you have your own milk, then I'm guessing there are not enough hours in the day to make many different varieties and you will soon get used to the processes that work best for you.

You are an important factor in cheese-making; it is a partnership between you, bacteria and milk. Try to be accurate and gentle, work confidently and easily, and remember: you will have a number of disasters on the way – everybody does. But perhaps you might learn from some of mine, which is why I'm included some of them on the next page...

Disasters

My very first cheese had a horrid taint that put me off the whole process of cheese-making. A chemist by training, I was under the misapprehension that all chemical reactions were more or less instant. They aren't.

I added my rennet to the milk at 28°C and thought that it should go off; after all, the recipe stated that four drops were enough. Yet when you're adding four tiny drops to 4.5 litres of milk, it doesn't seems to be enough somehow. By the time I had added half a bottle of rennet (say about 25 drops), the cheese had set and I went through the other stages.

The cheese looked good – but it didn't taste good at all.

Too high a temperature has also been a problem. Once, I heated milk well above 40°C by accident, then turned off the heat. The hob was still hot, however, and after a cooling period I added the rennet. Although I had learned my lesson about not adding too much rennet, this time nothing happened – nothing at all. I had denatured the rennet by adding hot milk. What I learned from this is that rennet is a protein and, like all proteins, it starts to break down at temperatures above 40°C.

Yet another disaster with hot milk occurred when I was making paneer. The recipe called for vinegar and a high temperature of 80°C. My milk must have been nearly at the boiling point, for when I added the vinegar, it turned straight away, but the nature of the curds was so fine that I couldn't do anything with them. I ended up with slurry.

My final big mistake was to think that slightly coagulated milk meant that the rennet had done its work. Pouring slurry into a muslin was quite off-putting!

These days, once I've made my cheese, someone in the house always comes along and eats it. Everyday cheese-making is more a question of what you need; making cheeses for show, or just for the complete bliss of eating your own speciality cheese, takes a little more care and work. Persevere, though, and you'll have success either way.

HARD CHEESE STEP BY STEP

Use the following steps for all cheeses, more or less, in different ways and proportions. If you are going to make large quantities of cheese, then you should try to control the acidity and make cheeses to the same pH every time. Use litmus papers to test the milk, if you like, but on the whole, home cheese producers don't have to worry too much about acidity.

Making cheese with vinegar uses an obvious excess of acid, but you don't have to test it; copious washing removes most of it, and it certainly gets rid of all the vinegar smell.

Ripening

It is odd that 'ripening' should come first as a cheese-making stage; however, milk has to be made ready for the various other processes involved. Ripening milk is normally the result of an increase in acidity as bacteria turns the sugar into lactic acid (see page 14). It occurs in the following stages.

Heating Heat the milk to the specified temperature – say 32°C, although each recipe will have its own temperature requirements.

Adding the starter When the milk has been at the correct temperature for a few minutes, add the starter. It is usual either to mix the starter with some of the milk, or cooled, boiled water.

Ripening period Leave the milk to rest in a warm place for 30–60 minutes. This allows you to control the amount of acidity in the milk. If it ripens for too long, the curds might leak when in the final cheese. This is what causes some cheeses to sit in their own milk on the shelf or in a plastic packet. Also, the cheese will taste too sharp.

Rennet

This enzyme works most efficiently at 38°C but it doesn't have to as long as you don't get the temperature higher than that. The most important thing is to be sure to use only *the specified amount* of rennet. If your milk has ripened properly, then you will have no problems getting a good set.

The coagulation of milk and the setting of curds are not the same thing. When milk coagulates, that is only half the story. Setting will take two to three times the length of time needed to start coagulation. Wait for the milk almost to solidify, like blancmange. Carefully thrust a sterile knife into the cheese; if it has set, it will give you a clean break where the milk splits and it won't (forgive me) look like baby sick.

Top stirring

If you're making cheese from cows milk, after warming the milk, allow it to stand; the butter-fat should rise to the top of the pan a little. When you add the rennet, stir it into this fatty layer a little first by gently stirring the top couple of centimetres with the flat action of a ladle. This produces a creamier cheese.

Cutting the curds

Once your cheese has set – after around 20 minutes or so – cut the curds into cubes in a crisscross fashion and then cut them diagonally from all sides. Aim to make pieces less than a centimetre across. This increases the surface area of the curds, allowing more whey to drain out. Curds more or less fall out of the suspension and you'll get clear liquid in the pan.

Cooking the curds

Some recipes call for the heat to be turned up at this stage, cooking the curds. This is often done by use of a water jacket or double boiler, less often under direct heat.

It is important that the curds aren't heated rapidly, so bring them up to temperature, usually around 40°C, over 15 minutes or so. Rapid heating causes them to lose fat, shrivel, become rubbery and almost impossible to press.

The basic idea is to force out the whey gently, losing as little fat from the curds as possible. During the cooking it is necessary to gently (GENTLY!) stir the curds to stop them from sticking.

Milling

Milling is simply the process of gently rubbing the curds between your fingers, then adding the required amount of salt. This removes much of the whey from the cheese and is particularly important when making some hard cheeses. When milling, you must be absolutely sure that your hands – especially your fingernails – are completely clean. Remember also, your cheese can take up taints from your fingers. If it is possible to wear sterile gloves, do so.

Draining

The curds are drained as normal, in a tied muslin bag. Hard cheeses are drained for about an hour, then the curds are put into a mould lined with muslin and pressed.

Salting

Salt slows or stops the development of the bacteria in cheese, which means that it all but halts a cheese's development at this point. I prefer to add salt after the draining process so that any extra whey that comes out of the cheese can then be easily drained off. Most recipes in this book will tell you either to salt to taste or to add 1–2% salt by weight. This means weighing your cheese and adding the appropriate amount. Where a percentage is specified, you can substitute 'salt to taste' if you like. In any case, I've kept the salt as low as possible, and as always, it is easier (and safer) to add too little salt and adjust to taste later. Some cheeses have a specific measured salt content, which should be adhered to.

Feta and Gouda cheeses are brined instead of straight-salted. This is done by dissolving 300g of salt in 1 litre of water and putting the cheese into this once it has been pressed. Be warned, though: unless your curds are really strong, your cheese might have difficulty withstanding the brining process, and the texture can break up.

Pressing

Cheeses can be pressed simply, between boards. To make hard cheese, however, you have to apply quite a lot of pressure, but not all at once. Making cheese commercially involves a measured pressure which increases over a period of 24 hours, but in the home you simply press a little at first, then harder later. It's best to have a Dutch press for this: you set it to press one notch for 12 hours, then to the next for another 12 hours.

Drying

Cheese that has been pressed is then allowed to air dry. Air drying turns cheese into something special, because as the cheese dries, its flavours mature. It also forms a skin.

Cheese is dried by removing it from both the mould and the cheesecloth, then turning it over a period of days. Use a cheese mat and turn the cheese a few times each day to keep it from sticking or breaking up, or remaining wet on one side and not the other. Always wear plastic gloves, or use a sterile palette knife to avoid your touching the cheese too much. This process can take place in the fridge, but remember: refrigerators are not always the most sterile of places, so be sure not to contaminate your cheese.

If you notice any mould growth on the cheese's surface, don't panic; simply sprinkle it with salt and then rub it away with a brined, sterile cloth. I tend to sprinkle the whole of the outside of the cheese with salt to deter mould growth – other than the ones I need, of course, which brings me neatly to…

Inoculating

It is usually at this stage that any desired ageing fungi are added to the surface of the cheese to make a Brie or Camembert, or using a blue mould to make a Roquefort. The process is simple: moulds are bought freeze-dried, then diluted in cooled, boiled water. You then spray this over the cheese.

It usually takes a fortnight for a mould to do its work. If you're making a blue cheese, it is usual practice to pierce it with a sterile skewer because the mould reacts with oxygen to produce the characteristic blue-cheese colour and flavour.

Bandaging

Hard cheeses such as Cheddar can be 'bandaged', which means wrapping them firmly but not too tightly with a a length of muslin. Bandaging slows evaporation and allows mould to form on the bandage, which slows evaporation even more. This way you get a

strong-flavoured cheese that is moist and succulent. A really useful method for preventing evaporation is to keep the bandaged cheese in the fridge, preferably in a container that you can open every day to change the atmosphere.

Waxing

Any cheese less than 1kg in weight can dry out more quickly than you'd wish. Some, like Parmesan, have a thick rind which helps prevent this, but waxing keeps a cheese free from infection as well as from becoming overly dry.

You can apply wax with a brush or by dipping. It is best done if the cheese is cooled beforehand, but like everything to do with cheeses, cool it slowly.

Melt the wax in a water bath and store any that is unused in a sterile plastic lidded box for next time. Give the cheese two thin coats – and that's all. Use a natural bristle brush rather than a plastic one; the latter may melt in the wax.

To be completely honest, I rarely bandage or wax my cheeses because they are consumed so quickly. My everyday cheese-making is confined to cottage cheese made for salads, paneer-type cheeses for cooking, and maybe the odd creamy Lancashire that has had a light pressing. But every now and then it is good to have a full-blown cheese-making session for these harder types.

Making cheese in batches

I don't have the room or the equipment in my kitchen to make huge batches of cheese in a semi-artisan way. Consequently, it isn't possible for me to set several gallons of milk in one go. Yet making hard cheese is usually better if you can set a couple of gallons of milk. Due to lack of space, I tend to set one gallon, then another, and possibly at times a third, then combine the curds at draining time, one after another.

The only problem with this method is finding a mould big enough to fit a kilo of cheese. Actually it's no problem at all, given that most cheese suppliers will clamour to sell you one.

Ageing

Ageing can take just a few days – indeed all cheeses should be allowed to rest for at least a few days – or up to several months. For the most part, however, the series of reactions that develop flavour over a period of weeks and months are slow, and it may seem that cheese, as it ages, is rotting away, becoming less edible day after day.

Poor-quality cheeses are like this; they might have all kinds of undesirable moulds and growths evolving in them. But if you have salted properly, if you have allowed your starter to develop and if you have been scrupulously clean throughout the cheese-making process, then the starter bacteria in the cheese release acid, which in turn inhibits the growth of other, more dangerous bacteria – and consequently preserves your cheese.

Most cheeses for home use are aged in old, disused but perfectly sterile refrigerators. They make an idea home (unplugged) for cheeses. The temperature doesn't vary and the humidity is fairly constant, and both are easily controlled by opening and closing the door.

Cheese needs to age at around 15°C and in 75% relative humidity. Hard cheeses are aged for around six months. During this time, the flavour will develop immensely. Check for cracks appearing on the surface, which mean the cheese is drying out. If they appear, fill them with a little butter, which will also help moisturise the cheese, and place a dish containing a little water nearby to increase the humidity.

SOFT CHEESES

What I mean by 'soft cheeses' are those that you can easily spread on bread – i.e. that are soft enough not to be sliced. The simplest soft cheese is made from yoghurt that has been allowed to ripen for a day past its sell-by date. Add 5g salt per litre to draw out the whey from the cheese – and the whey takes most of the salt with it. You then ladle the curds into a cheesecloth and hang it to allow the whey to drain.

The result is quite a wet, soft cheese that will spread very easily and keep for a week. It makes a great ingredient to include in a pasta dish, and as always, you can add herbs of your choice to vary the flavour.

Boursin

Boursin is one of those cheeses you either love or hate. For years I didn't realise it was made from horseradish; instead, I reckoned it was made from added garlic. Be careful with horseradish: although this recipe calls for 5g, try just 1g first and see what you think about the flavour; only then should you progress to a stronger cheese. Remember, horseradish brings tears to the eyes more than any other herb, so remember to wash your hands.

5 litres milk
1 sachet mesophillic starter
4 drops rennet, mixed in 1–2 tablespoons cooled, boiled water
2g salt
5g grated horseradish
1 clove garlic, grated

1. Pour the milk into a large pan and warm it to 30°C, then add the starter. Leave it to work for 45 minutes.

2. Add the rennet and stir carefully.

3. Allow the cheese to stand while the curds form, then let it stand for 12 hours.

4. Carefully place the curds into cheesecloth (try to keep it in one whole 'curd'), then pull the corners together and hang it for 12 hours to drain off the whey.

5. Add the salt, grated horseradish and garlic and mix well, then pack the cheese into ramekins and keep refrigerated.

Cottage Cheese

You can't get any more basic than cottage or curd cheese. It is so basic, in fact, that you're probably copying the very first cheese-makers in the art of cheese-making. The simplest cottage cheese can be made with as little as half a litre (1 pint) of milk. This small amount means that it's also possible to collect various milk dregs and make cheese from them in the following way: bring the milk to the boil, then let it cool a little, then add 1 tablespoon of lemon juice per 500ml and the curds will separate from the whey. Simply collect the curds into a muslin square and allow them to drain. Salt to taste, and you have a perfectly acceptable cottage cheese. You can use also use vinegar to curdle the milk, but it imparts a vinegary flavour. Counter this by washing the curds – but be careful. If your curds are fine-grained, you might wash them away, so instead, simply stand the muslin in repeated changes of water. If the curds are robust, however, just wash them carefully in gently running water. Of course, washing the curds might mean they are not so flavoursome, so you might want to add cream or another flavour to the cheese. To make a more sophisticated cottage cheese using a starter and rennet, follow the recipe below. This cheese will take any flavours, and can easily be lightly pressed into a tablet.

5 litres fresh milk
1 sachet mesophillic starter
5 drops rennet
Cheesecloth

1. Pour the milk into a large pan and warm it to 28°C, then add the starter. Allow the milk to cool slowly to room temperature – so wait at least an hour before you add the rennet.

3. Cover the pan and set aside overnight at 20°C. To keep the temperature constant, remove the pan from any heat source and wrap it in a clean towel (or simply leave it, covered, in a warm part of the kitchen).

4. Cut the curd into 1cm cubes and heat to 40°C. Cook at this temperature for 45 minutes, stirring carefully every 5 minutes or so. The curds will shrivel a little and 'fall' in the whey.

5. Line a colander with cheesecloth and drain the curds for 15 minutes, then transfer them to a muslin square and hang until they stop dripping.

6. Place in a bowl and salt to taste.

Cream Cheese

These are the recipes I use when making a proper cream cheese. I think Jerseys are the best cows for full-fat milk: you get a lot of golden-coloured cream and the flavour is divine.

5 litres milk (the creamier the better)
1 sachet mesophillic starter
4 drops rennet
Salt

1. Pour the milk into a large pan and heat it to 25°C. Add the starter, then leave to stand for 45 minutes before adding the rennet. Cover the pan and leave it in a warm place for 12 hours so that the curds will set.

2. Gently transfer the set curd, whole, into a muslin square, then draw up the corners and hang it to drain for 12 hours.

3. Return the curd to a pan and mix in salt to taste; this will draw out more whey, so hang the muslin again until the curds stop dripping.

Extra-creamy Cream Cheese

This very creamy cheese should last five days, but in our house we eat it very quickly!

1 litre whole milk
1 litre double cream, at room temperature
100ml mesophillic starter solution
2 tablespoons lemon juice

1. Warm the milk to 40°C. Add the cream, slowly reduce the temperature to 30°C, then add the starter. Take the pan off the heat, leave it for 45 minutes, then add the lemon juice.

2. Drain the cheese into a colander lined with at least 2 layers of cheesecloth. Tie up the corners and hang it for at least 12 hours, or until the drips have stopped. Transfer to the fridge in a sealed container.

Roule Cheese

This is as much a way of presenting a cheese as it is a recipe. The cheese is spread out, then rolled up like a Swiss roll. Admittedly, sometimes this doesn't work, but if it doesn't, simply mash it all together: you'll still have a great-flavoured cheese suitable for spreading.

5 litres milk
1 sachet mesophillic starter
5 drops rennet, mixed in 1–2 tablespoons cooled, boiled water
Salt to taste
1 tablespoon cream
Garlic or chopped herbs to taste
Cracked peppercorns or sesame seeds

1. Pour the milk in a pan and heat it to 30°C. Add the starter. Remove from the heat, wait 45 minutes, then add the rennet, stirring well.

2. Leave to stand for 45 minutes, then cut the curds into 1cm cubes and drain them in a colander lined with a cheesecloth.

3. Ladle the curds into another sheet of cheesecloth, hang up to drain.

4. Add salt to taste, which will also draw out more whey, so be sure to hang the curds again to allow it to drain.

5. Transfer the curds to a dish and add a tablespoon of cream; mix it into a light paste. This stage can be omitted if you want a firmer (but less creamy) cheese.

6. Add any herbs you wish, but not too many: flavours can be easily 'confused' or overwhelming. A few snips of chives work, as does 1 grated garlic clove, or even some chopped sage.

7. Spoon out the cheese onto a piece of cling film (or wet muslin will do), then sprinkle the surface with crushed peppercorns so that it forms a dark layer (sesame seeds add a nutty flavour).

8. Carefully roll up the cheese into a log, like a Swiss roll, then slice it and store it, covered, in the fridge.

CHEDDAR

The *Oxford English Dictionary* says Cheddar cheese is named for Cheddar, England, and thus gives it a capital 'C', but the name also refers to a process called 'cheddaring', which is a way of draining off whey by piling cut curds on top of each other. The method listed in this chapter doesn't rely on cheddaring as such, but it does produce a good example of the cheese. First made in Elizabethan times, Cheddar has travelled the world, picking up all kinds of unusual names in the process: Flat, Twin of Longhorn in the USA, Black Diamond in Australia.

Cheddar is a high-fat cheese with a yellowish colour, often with a good rind. Homemade Cheddar is wrapped to help it mature, and sometimes it can be so acidic and strong it will make your mouth sore. However, ageing Cheddar for more than a couple of months (but less than five) yields a great cheese.

Both the recipes that follow simulate the cheddaring process of cutting curds into fairly large blocks, which are then stacked on top of each other to drain off the whey. They are restacked frequently, in order. The stacking is usually three curd blocks high, the lowermost being put on top and the other two moved down until every block has had half an hour on the bottom. Then the curds are milled to a smaller size.

The art of making a good Cheddar is not to lose all the fat content while at the same time getting as much whey out of the cheese as possible. Fat has many roles to play here, and it is important in terms of flavour, but a cheese's structure depends on fat, too. If it weren't so fatty, it wouldn't get that smooth consistency Cheddar is so famous for.

Some people add colouring to the milk before the renneting stage. If you choose to, use a cheese dye made specifically for that purpose.

Easy Cheddar

This easy recipe makes an acceptable Cheddar in a short length of time, providing you with a really great result – ideal to show off at parties, or just to have on hand in the kitchen as a store-cupboard hard cheese. This recipe calls for nine litres (about two gallons), but if you have a small pan, you can make it in two batches, then combine the curds. The required rate of rennet is one drop per litre, so it is just as easy to either add ten drops or two lots of five.

9 litres full-fat milk
1 standard-sized sachet freeze-dried mesophillic starter
10 drops rennet
3–4 tablespoons cheese salt
Cheese wax

1. In a large pan, heat the milk to exactly 32°C.

2. Add the starter and stir well, then cover and keep warm for 45 minutes away from the heat. (If making two batches, make sure to add the appropriate amount of starter and rennet to each).

3. Dilute the rennet in a few tablespoons of cool, boiled, unchlorinated water. Stir it into the milk and starter mixture carefully for 1 minute, then leave to stand for another 45 minutes at 32°C. The easiest way to achieve this temperature is to take the pan off the heat, then cover it with a towel. Another way is to give it a blast of heat, then remove it. Either way, the nearest you can keep it to 32°C, the better.

4. Cut the curds into 1cm pieces, then place the pan into a water bath and very slowly increase the temperature to 38°C. As the temperature rises, stir the curds. Make sure they don't stick together. They will slowly decrease in size and darken to a creamy yellow colour.

5. When the temperature reaches 38°C, leave the curds to stand on the heat for 10 minutes before gently pouring them into a muslin-lined colander.

6. Hang the curds in the muslin until they stop dripping. While hanging, try to keep the cheese warm, avoiding draughts.

7. Carefully pour the curds into a bowl and break them in half with your fingers, then add the cheese salt. If you have made this cheese in two batches, now is the time to combine them.

8. Line a mould with cheesecloth and place the curds into it. Put a 5kg weight on top, or apply 5kg of pressure for 15 minutes. Turn the cheese over in the mould, then press with 10kg for 15 minutes.

9. Turn again and press for six hours at 15kg, then give it a final turn and press at 15kg for a final six hours.

10. Remove the cheese from the mould and leave it to dry for a few days on a cheese mat. Ensure that it is free from contamination during this period.

11. Apply cheese wax with a bristle brush, then leave it to age for at least a month at 15°C and 75% relative humidity.

Stirred-curd Cheddar

9 litres full-fat milk
1 standard-sized sachet freeze-dried mesophillic starter
13–14 drops rennet
3–4 tablespoons cheese salt
Cheese wax

1. Follow steps 1–3 in the Easy Cheddar recipe on page 66.

2. Cut the curds into small pieces – around half a centimetre in size. Leave them to settle for 10 minutes or so before placing the pan in a water bath and slowly heating them to 38°C.

3. When at temperature, gently stir the curds for 30 minutes, then drain them into a muslin-lined colander and add the salt. Do not turn the curds in any way, just combine the salt with them gently. This will remove a lot of the whey.

4. Stir every 5 minutes, then return the cheese to the pan, cover and leave it over a low heat for 1 hour at 38°C.

5. Pour into a muslin-lined colander and follow steps 6–11 in the Easy Cheddar recipe on page 67 to finish.

AMERICAN-STYLE CHEDDARS

What people call 'American cheese' varies in many ways. It is widely understood to be what we in the UK would call 'processed cheese', but this is selling the term short. There is another American cheese that resembles a rich Cheddar. It also provides a reasonably high yield of cheese from just five litres (about one gallon) of milk with some milk powder added.

American Cheddar No 1

Possibly the best way of making a hard cheese for everyday use.

5 litres full-fat milk
200g good-quality milk powder
250ml plain yoghurt
250ml single cream
5 drops rennet
2 teaspoons cheese salt

1. Add the first 4 ingredients to a large pan and warm the mixture to 30°C. Leave this to stand on the heat for a couple of hours, stirring now and again to be sure everything is mixed.

2. Add the rennet and leave it to stand until the curds give a clean cut: about 45–60 minutes.

3. Cut the curds into 1cm cubes and slowly, over a period of 30 minutes, increase the temperature to 40°C.

4. Keep the curds at 40°C for 30 minutes, then ladle them into a cheesecloth. Hang until they have stopped dripping.

5. Press the curds under moderate pressure (about 5–10kg) for 12 hours. There is no need to change or turn the cheese.

6. Place the cheese on a cheese mat to dry, turning it over a couple of times every day to ensure even evaporation.

Colby Cheese

This American take on Cheddar is often dyed and is always softer than Cheddar. It is an example of a washed cheese, where the curds are washed at the cooking stage.

9 litres full-fat milk
1 standard-sized sachet freeze-dried mesophillic starter
10 drops rennet
3–4 tablespoons cheese salt
Cheese wax

1. Follow the recipe for Easy Cheddar on page 66 through step 5, where the curds are cooking at 38°C for 10 minutes.

2. Carefully ladle out the whey and replace it with water that has been boiled and allowed to cool to room temperature. This cooling water allows the cheese to become moist.

3. Press the cheese as per the Easy Cheddar recipe on page 67 and you can wax it, too, if you prefer. It will age for 2 months and you will be surprised at how creamy it has become.

FLAVOURED CHEDDARS

Cheddar can be enhanced in various ways to make unusually different flavours. This involves adding liquids to the milk before setting the cheese. Add only around 125ml of liquid, and then, in order to make up for the mildly diluted milk, add another drop or two of rennet. In fact, the dilution is so small that there is no real difference in the rennet stage, but some liquids will reduce the efficiency of rennet. Use either of the Cheddar recipes on pages 66–68 as the basis for the following cheeses.

Guinness Cheese

This cheese was very popular a few years ago and sold in shops, although I haven't seen it for some time. I used to make it with a litre of Guinness, but that is too much beer to waste – which is why this recipe leaves more for drinking! (Actually it creates a more uniform flavour than the old method.)

1. Take half a glass of Guinness and leave it overnight to go flat. Give it a good stir and, once completely flat, place it in a pan and heat it to a low simmer. Reduce the Guinness by half, then leave it to cool completely. The flavour will have intensified and is probably completely disgusting to taste as a drink, so don't be tempted to try it!

2. Stir this into the milk at the beginning of your Cheddar recipe, then follow the recipe as standard.

Sage Cheddar

This used to be known as Lincoln Green, for obvious reasons. Sage reduces the efficiency of the starter, however, so add this liquid only after the milk has ripened and before you add rennet. As a natural antibiotic, sage actually keeps the cheese free from infection, but it also alters its microbial content, so there is little point in keeping it for months. You can use this up fairly quickly – say a month after making. Any ageing after that provides only a negligible improvement in flavour.

1. Take a handful of fresh sage and chop it finely. Add this to a cup of boiling water and simmer for 10–15 minutes.

2. Strain the sage and add the cooled sage water to the milk after it has ripened but before adding the rennet, then follow the Cheddar recipe.

Caraway Cheddar

You can make another herb Cheddar by steeping caraway seeds in water.

1. Steep 1 tablespoon of caraway seeds for 2 hours in 125ml (half a cup) cool water.

2. Strain the seeds, then add the flavoured water to the milk before ripening and follow the Cheddar recipe.

FLAVOURING THE CURDS

These cheeses are made by adding flavouring to Cheddar curds before pressing so that it is evenly spread through the cheese.

Marmite Cheese

A very easy recipe. Any excess liquid is removed during the pressing stage.

1. Dribble a tablespoon of marmite through the curds. Don't mix it in; simply carefully draw the curds together for pressing so that the cheese will be veined.

2. Leave for a week before eating. Don't age this one for long, and don't wax the cheese.

Onion/Sage and Onion

To be sure the onion and sage are as clean as possible, use spring onions, finely chopped, and sage leaves without any woody or connective tissue. If you've made cheese with 5 litres of milk, use about 25g spring onions for onion-flavoured cheese and about 5g sage for sage and onion.

1. Drop the finely chopped ingredients into boiling water for just a few seconds, then remove to dry before use.

2. When the curds are ready, sprinkle the onions and herbs among them, then press in the normal way.

Garlic Cheese

Only use fresh garlic for this variation – never garlic salt.

1. Chop a single clove of garlic and mix it completely with the curds before pressing. Garlic is also a natural antibiotic, and this will have an effect on the starter bacteria. There is no need to age this cheese; simply leave it for a few days to dry.

CHEDDAR-LIKE CHEESES

Derby Cheese

This traditional Derbyshire cheese is similar to Cheddar, but it is much moister and has a slightly flaky texture. Sage Derby was made by adding a mixture of finely chopped sage leaves steeped in water. A traditional Christmas cheese, the sage helped keep the cheese for as long as it was needed – often until the spring, when new calves were born – so this is a true cottager's cheese.

This recipe makes a cheese that is lighter than Cheddar because it isn't heated as high. You can make it in two batches of 4.5 litres each. Derby will mature for three months. It will break apart more easily than Cheddar and have a slightly nuttier flavour.

9 litres full-fat milk
1 packet mesophillic starter
10 drops rennet
3–4 level tablespoons cheese salt

1. Heat the milk to 28°C exactly. Add the starter and stir well. Cover and keep the cheese at 28°C for 1 hour, then add the rennet and leave for another hour until you have a clean break.

2. Cut the curds into 1cm pieces. Put the pan in a water bath, then slowly heat the curds to 34°C, stirring them every few minutes. Cook for 20 minutes at this temperature.

3. Carefully put the curds into a muslin-lined colander and leave them to drain. Cover with a lid or a very clean towel to keep the temperature as steady as possible.

4. Carefully pour the curds into a bowl and break them into smaller pieces with your fingers, then add the salt. If you have made this cheese in two batches, now is the time to combine them.

5. Line a mould with cheesecloth and place the curds into it. Press with a 5kg weight or apply 5kg of pressure for 15 minutes. Remove the cheese, turn it over and press with 10kg for 15 minutes. Turn again and press for 6 hours at 15kg, then turn it again and give it a final pressing at 15kg for 12 hours. Remove it from the mould and leave it to dry for a few days on a cheese mat. Ensure that it is free from contamination during this period.

6. Age it for at least a month at 15°C and 75% relative humidity.

Red Leicester Cheese

Formerly made in the same dairies as Stilton, this cheese was originally coloured with carrot juice. Nowadays, of course, you can buy the appropriate colouring from cheese suppliers. Some recipes call for the juice of a lemon to go in with the starter to add flavour; however, you can make it sharper by adding lemon juice once the curds have been set.

1. Follow the recipe for Derby Cheese (opposite), but add just 2 drops of cheese colouring per 5 litres to the milk as you add the starter, stirring well.

2. Salt to taste using cheese salt, then give the final pressed cheese a dusting of salt to enhance its flavour as it ages.

BLUE CHEESE

Blue cheese is a result of the fungus *Penicillium roqueforti*, which not only converts sugars, alters texture and adds various interesting flavours to the cheese, it reacts with oxygen to create a blue vein. It is this blue vein, along with increased acidity, that concentrates the flavour of the cheese.

Penicillium roqueforti needs salt to grow well, so these cheeses are generally slightly saltier than normal. Adding the fungus is best done via an atomiser or hand spray, into which you put the required amount of mould in a specified amount of water. This sounds vague, but different suppliers specify different amounts, so always read the instructions on the packet.

In the past I have cheated when making blue cheese in the following way: take a fresh, new piece of blue cheese – you don't need much – and add half to a fresh Cheddar (the Easy Cheddar recipe on page 66 is great for this) you are pressing. You don't need any *Penicillium roqueforti*; instead, just wait for the fungus in the existing blue to work its way through the new cheese. This process usually takes a month, by which time your Cheddar has aged properly, too.

Blue cheese can be made from all kinds of milk: the French *bleu de chèvre* uses goats milk, the British blue Stilton uses cows milk, while Roquefort is made from ewes milk.

Danish Blue

5 litres really creamy full-fat milk
1 sachet mesophillic starter
1g (⅛ teaspoon) *Penicillium roqueforti*
6 drops rennet mixed in 1–2 tablespoons cooled, boiled water
1 level teaspoon salt

1. Mix the milk and starter together in a pan, then heat to 34°C. Remove from the heat and leave for 1 hour to ripen.

2. Add the *Penicillium roqueforti*, then the rennet. Make sure everything is well-mixed.

3. Allow the cheese to cool a little, but keep it out of draughts and don't let it cool rapidly.

4. Cut the curds to 4cm cubes and allow to rest for another hour.

5. Pour off the whey and carefully transfer the curds into a cheesecloth-lined colander. Drain for 20 minutes, then sprinkle with the salt.

6. Spoon the curds into a cheesecloth-lined mould and very lightly press them, just at hand pressure. Then put the cheese into a plastic container in the fridge and, after a week, sprinkle the surface with salt and pierce it all over with a needle.

7. Leave for a fortnight to mature, and check to see if there are blue moulds developing. If it smells bad, however, don't taste it – discard it immediately and put it down to experience!

Blue Stilton

All Stilton cheeses are rich, and this blue version of the famous platter cheese is fantastic. It is very creamy and has a wonderful flavour. Be vigilant about hygiene throughout the cheese-making process: you don't want to introduce any microbes into your blue that would make it go bad.

100ml good cream
1 sachet mesophillic starter
5 litres full-fat milk
5 drops rennet
1g (⅛ teaspoon) *Penicillium roqueforti*
3–4 level teaspoons salt

1. Combine the cream, starter and milk and warm it slowly until it reaches 30°C. Stir regularly so that everything is mixed well. Remove from the heat and let it stand for 1 hour.

2. Add the rennet and stir well. Leave for 45 minutes until you have a clean break in the curds.

3. Cut the curds into 1cm blocks, then leave them to stand for 15 minutes. Ladle them into a cheesecloth, tie up the corners and hang it for 1 hour.

4. Open the cheesecloth and add the salt. Form the cheese into a ball, then wash it with *Penicillium roqueforti* dissolved in some water (about ⅛ teaspoon per 100ml).

5. Moulding is a two-stage process. First, pack the inoculated curds into muslin-lined cheese moulds and press lightly for 12 hours either with a 10kg weight on top or with 10kg of pressure in a cheese press. Next, place the cheese on a sterile mat and turn it over every day for a week. Rub a little vegetable oil onto the surface, then leave it for another week.

6. Pierce the cheese all over with a sterile needle. The blue mould should form a couple of weeks later, and your cheese should be ready to eat after 3 weeks.

Roquefort

Roquefort is an ancient cheese that has been made for well over 2,000 years. This recipe approximation produces an excellent, creamy cheese because it contains a high level of fat and protein, and the milk is very forgiving. In essence, this is a little like the Easy Cheddar recipe on page 66, but uses ewes milk instead of cows milk. I have reduced the temperatures in order to keep as much of the fat as possible in the curds.

9 litres whole ewes milk
1 sachet freeze-dried mesophillic starter
1g (⅛ teaspoon) *Penicillium roqueforti*
10 drops rennet
3–4 tablespoons cheese salt
Cheese wax

1. Pour the milk into a pan and heat it to 30°C.

2. Add the starter and *Penicillium roqueforti* and stir well, then cover and keep warm for 45 minutes, away from the heat.

3. Dilute the rennet in a few tablespoons of cool, boiled, unchlorinated water. Stir it into the milk mixture carefully for 1 minute, then take it off the heat, cover the pan with a towel and leave to stand for another 45 minutes at 30°C.

4. Cut the curds into 1cm pieces, then leave them for 10 minutes before gently pouring them into a muslin-lined colander.

5. Gather up the corners of the muslin and hang the curds until they stop dripping. Try to keep the cheese warm, avoiding draughts.

6. Carefully pour the curds into a bowl, break them in half with your fingers, then pour in the salt.

7. Line a mould with cheesecloth and place the curds into it. Press for 6 hours at 15kg of pressure (or use a 15kg weight), then turn the cheese over and give it a final pressing at 15kg for 6 hours.

8. Remove the cheese from the mould and leave it to dry for a few days on a cheese mat. Ensure that it is free from contamination during this period and sprinkle it with a little salt.

9. Place the cheese in a container, and after a week, pierce it all over with a sterile needle.

10. Mature for at least 6 weeks before eating.

GOATS CHEESE

Caproic and caprylic fatty acids in goats milk contribute to the flavour of goats milk cheese. Some people (myself included) cannot abide it, whereas others are enthusiastic to the extreme. However, many studies have shown goats milk to be the nearest animal milk to human breast milk, and it is certainly perfectly safe for human consumption.

Goats milk cheese is probably the oldest cheese in the world, and it was traditionally heavily salted. Modern goats milk cheese doesn't need to be, however, and as such, it is very suitable for people recovering from illnesses – especially for anyone who suffers with certain kidney problems. It does, though, require careful handling.

The curds produced by goats milk are generally softer than those made from cows milk, and the resulting cheese is also higher in acidity and has the tendency to pick up taints of various kinds. It is the size of the fat particles that makes goats milk white, as well as the fact that the animals don't pass on carotene in their milk, so you get a very pure, white cheese.

Some people (and many cheese-making books) add colourant to goats milk cheese, but I cannot think why.

HOW TO MAKE GOOD GOATS CHEESE

Even more so than when making any type of cheese, it is important to keep your preparation area free from aromas as well as spotlessly clean when making goats cheese. If you're wearing rubber gloves or have splashed the perfume about too much, the milk will taint, and if you store the cheese in a container that has a smell, then the cheese will pick up that smell, too.

Equally, be sure that your measurements are accurate and that you never rush the process. Temperature control is an important skill, as is using the right quantity of ingredients. Always use fresh rennet and starters and don't try to 'make do' with old or badly stored ingredients. Similarly, use fresh milk – don't store it.

The curd-cutting stage is the time you're most likely to have a problem; because of the more fragile nature of goats-milk curds, they might fall apart or simply disappear. Once you have cut the curds – a task that calls for gentleness – leave them to stand for a quarter of an hour to be sure they firm up before increasing the temperature to cook them. This way you should get a decent cheese.

Rennet-free Goats Cheese

*It might take more than a day to collect this amount of goats milk, but be scrupulously
clean if you store the milk for any length of time before using.*

5 litres fresh goats milk
Juice of 4 lemons
Salt to taste

1. In a large pan, heat the milk to 60°C.

2. Add the lemon juice. If there isn't enough acidity – which you'll know if the curds haven't
formed – add the juice of another lemon.

3. Let the curds stand and allow the mixture to cool to 40°C. Note: you might not have a lot
in the way of curds; it could turn out to be just a messy-looking mixture, and in this case you
should leave it to settle, ladling the whey off as it appears.

4. If you can, cut the curd into 1cm cubes and gently pour them into a cheesecloth-lined
colander. Otherwise, add the mass to the colander, gently and without bashing the cheese too
much. Draw together the corners of the cloth and hang it up to drain the whey.

5. Leave the curds to drain for 1 hour. You'll get a ricotta-type cheese that can be sweetened
and used in dessert dishes. Alternatively, hang it for 4 hours and you can then add cream to
it and make a cream-cheese product.

6. Add salt to taste, place in an odourless container and leave it to age for 1 month. Give it
a light pressing after this time, if you wish, and you will have a crumbly cheese.

Chèvre

*Chèvre is the French version of goats cheese. You can buy special chèvre starters at
cheese-making suppliers. This cheese has a number of variations: you can lightly salt
it or add all kinds of herbs. Do note, however, that lightly salted, it will
last for only a week in the fridge.*

5 litres goats milk
Chèvre starter

1. Heat the milk to 30°C.

2. Add the starter and combine completely by stirring for a few minutes. Allow the milk to
cool to room temperature and cover, then keep it at room temperature for 12 or more hours.
The starter will have acidified the milk and curds.

3. Place the curds gently into a sheet of muslin and hang it to drain the whey. Hang for 12
hours for a cream-cheese-type consistency.

Rennet-based Goats Cheese

The following cheese was created as a teaching tool. You can alter this recipe to suit your own milk and herbs as well as your own way of making cheese. Eat within a week of making.

5 litres goats milk
1 sachet mesophillic starter
4 drops rennet

1. Heat the milk to 28°C and add the starter.

2. After 30 minutes, add the rennet and stir well. Cover and leave until you get a clean break in the curds. This could be many hours, though, and remember to handle the curds carefully; don't move the pan at all.

3. Carefully ladle the curds into muslin-lined cheese moulds and then stand them to drain.

4. Once fully drained, the cheese will have shrunk in the moulds and have a definite resistance to the touch. Gently sprinkle the curds with salt, then let them stand for 1 day.

Variations

Mi-Chèvre

This is made from a combination of goats and cows milk. It usually consists of 75% of the latter and is therefore more robust, and the goats milk passes on some of the flavour. You can also use this milk combination in any of the recipes in this book to make Mi-Chèvre.

Saint Maure

This cheese is rolled in black wood ash and is made with *Penicillium candidum*. Traditionally it is moulded into a platted straw to allow handling. Make the Rennet-based Goats Cheese above, but when the cheeses are removed from the moulds and have been salted, spray them all over with the bacteria (the mould doesn't work properly without salt) and leave them for a fortnight at room temperature. Keep the cheeses in a plastic container with a little water in a small bowl so that the humidity remains high.

Feta

This feta can be made from either ewes or goats milk, and is usually added to salads. The ubiquitous olives and feta salad uses a fairly bland cheese, but you can get some really strong ones if you experiment when making them yourself. Feta is made all over southeastern Europe, Greece, Bulgaria, Albania. Each country has its own little variations: some use specific starters, others simply use buttermilk, like the Bulgarian recipe below.

5 litres ewes or goats milk
450ml buttermilk
1 sachet mesophillic starter
6 drops rennet
Salt
Brine, made from 7g salt per litre of water

1. Heat the milk to 30°C. Add the buttermilk and starter.

2. Leave for an hour, stirring from time to time.

3. Add the rennet, then leave it to set 1 hour.

4. Cut into 1cm cubes and let stand for 20 minutes.

5. Ladle the curds and whey into feta moulds or a muslin-lined colander. Sprinkle with salt to taste and leave overnight to drain.

6. Remove the cheese from the mould and cut it into 1cm cubes.

7. Leave uncovered for 1 week, then cut the pieces again into 1cm cubes and store in the brine solution.

Goats Milk Ricotta

A good approximation of the unsalted Italian cheese. This version can be stored in the refrigerator for up to one week.

5 litres goats milk
70ml apple cider vinegar
100g unsalted butter, melted
½ teaspoon baking soda

1. Heat the milk to 80°C.

2. Keep it at this temperature for about 5 minutes, then slowly stir in the vinegar. The curds should begin to separate from the whey.

3. When you see the whey clearly in the pan, stop adding vinegar.

4. With a slotted spoon, gently ladle the curds into a colander lined with cheesecloth. Drain for 30 minutes, then transfer the curds into a bowl.

5. Gently stir in the melted butter and baking soda, then leave to set. It usually forms a big curd, but large or small, when set, you'll see it.

EUROPEAN CHEESES

It would be impossible in one book to cover all the cheeses that are actually produced in continental Europe, but this chapter is designed to provide you with a good introduction to those European-type cheeses you can make successfully at home. The reason for this selective attitude is that the subtle variations of European cheeses, particularly those from France, are not easily replicated in the home – and the focus of this book, after all, is on what you can make it in your own kitchen. Many cheeses need at least a small dairy in order to be able to create them.

This chapter includes cheese recipes derived from those made in both northern and southern Europe. Provided you can keep your temperatures constant and your equipment scrupulously clean, you should be able to make them all without any problem – and for much cheaper than you could buy them in the shops!

NORTHERN EUROPEAN CHEESES

Cheeses from Germany, Holland and Belgium and even more northerly climes have a distinctive rubberiness about them. There is also a huge variation in flavours and textures, and if you happen to be in Lapland, you might even get reindeer cheese (but they put it in tea, which never really works…).

The season for growing grass isn't as long in northern Europe as it is in the UK, but the result is still very rich. In the far north, the staple diet for grazing animals is lichen, and this is also reflected in the quality of the cheese.

Edam

Edam is the archetypal Dutch cheese: mild, interestingly creamy, and, yes, rubbery, though none the worse for that. It is made using thermophillic starters (see page 29). Capable of withstanding higher temperatures, the bacteria in these cultures are robust, and they produce a nutty flavour. They are also responsible for the cheese's texture, and scalding also gives it a rubbery feel. You don't have to wax Edam, but it keeps better if you do. Sometimes colourants are added, but I never bother.

5 litres fresh milk
1 sachet thermophillic starter
5 drops rennet
Salt to taste
Brine, made from 200g salt per litre of water

1. In a large pan, combine the milk with the starter at room temperature and slowly increase the temperature to 32°C. Keep the mixture at this temperature for 15 minutes.

2. Remove from the heat and leave to stand for 1 hour, letting it cool to room temperature. Mix the rennet in 1–2 tablespoons of cool, boiled water and add it to the mixture. Leave to stand for 1 hour, then cut the curds into 1cm cubes.

3. Put back on the heat and increase the temperature to 40°C while gently stirring the curds every now and then. Keep at 40°C for 30 minutes.

4. Remove from the heat and allow the curds to settle for 40 minutes, cooling to room temperature, then carefully pour off the whey.

5. Wash the curds in boiled water that has been allowed to cool to around 55°C; this is the scalding process. Leave them at this temperature for 15 minutes.

6. Line a colander with cheesecloth and drain the curds for 15 minutes. Salt to taste.

7. Press the cheese for 1 day on each side with a light pressure of around 5kg.

8. Soak the cheese in brine for 2 days, turning it over every few hours. Leave to dry, then coat it with cheese wax (red is traditional), and allow it to stand for a month before eating.

Emmental

This Swiss cheese has all the characteristics of Edam but with a harder texture, a stronger, nuttier flavour and holes. The culture Propionic Shermanii is responsible for its flavour, texture – and holes. During maturation, carbon dioxide is released into the cheese to create the holes. Emmental isn't waxed but simply allowed to mature in the air. This recipe calls for ten litres of milk, but you can make it in two batches and combine them if you like.

1 teaspoon *Propionic shermanii*
10 litres milk
1 sachet thermophillic starter
10 drops rennet
Brine, made from 300g salt per litre of water

1. Add the *Propionic shermanii* to a cup of the milk and mix well.

2. Pour the rest of the milk into a pan and heat to 32°C. Add the starter, then stir in the *Propionic shermanii* milk, remove the pan from the heat and keep it at this temperature for 30 minutes. Add the rennet, and continue to make sure the milk remains at 32°C.

3. Leave to stand on the heat for 45 minutes, by which time the curds should have formed. Continue to maintain the 32°C temperature and cut the curds into pea-sized pieces.

4. Slowly increase the temperature to 40°C over 10 minutes or so and keep the curds at this temperature for 15 minutes. Then cook the curds by slowly increasing the temperature to 45°C, and leave it there for 30 minutes.

5. Drain the curds and scald them as in the Edam recipe (see page 93, step 6).

6. Put the cheese under light pressure (5kg) overnight, then stand it in brine for 2 days.

7. Dry on a cheese mat and mature for a few days before eating.

Gouda

Although this Dutch cheese has some of the characteristics of Edam, it is actually quite different. This recipe calls for mesophillic starter; however, a pot of yoghurt works just as well.

10 litres milk
1 sachet mesophillic starter
10 drops rennet
Brine, made from 300g salt per litre of water
Cheese wax

1. In a large pan, heat the milk to 32°C and add the starter, keeping it at the temperature for 30 minutes.

2. Add the rennet and leave covered at 32°C for an hour. It is important that you get a clean break and hard curds.

3. Cut the curds into 1cm cubes and pour off half the whey.

4. Add hand-hot water until the temperature of the curds reaches 35°C.

5. Leave for 30 minutes, then increase the temperature to 38°C and leave them to set for 30 minutes.

6. Carefully ladle the curds into a cheesecloth-lined mould. Press for 30 minutes at 5kg. Turn the cheese over and repeat the pressing, then leave it under pressure overnight (or for at least 8 hours).

7. Stand the cheese in brine for half a day, then dry it on a cheese mat and coat with cheese wax.

Gruyère

Gruyère can be made from skimmed milk, and certain recipes call for skimmed evening milk and non-skimmed morning milk. This particular recipe can be troublesome; often you don't get the required holes, and it is much easier to make if you add a teaspoon of Propionic shermanii to the initial mixture. In the old days, however, warm temperatures made the holes: the higher temperature causes gas to be formed in the cheese, which breaks out, forming the holes. A word of caution: I don't like the idea of keeping cheese at high temperatures for long periods. I worry about what might be growing in it, so if you see any discolouration or bad smells in your homemade Gruyère, then discard it just to be on the safe side.

5 litres fresh milk
1 sachet thermophillic starter
6 drops rennet, mixed in 1–2 tablespoons cooled, boiled water
Brine, made from 200g salt per litre of water

1. Warm the milk to 32°C and add the starter, mixing well. Leave for 45 minutes.

2. Add the rennet and leave until you get a clean-break curd.

3. Over the course of an hour, heat the curds to 52°C, stirring all the time with a whisk. You should get small, pea-sized curds.

4. Drain the curds and sprinkle them with a level teaspoon of salt.

5. Press the curds into cheesecloth-lined moulds and press lightly (at about 5kg) for 12 hours.

6. Turn the cheese over and press lightly again for another 24 hours.

7. Float in a light brine for 2 days, then mature as follows: keep the cheese at around 20°C at 85% humidity for 5 weeks, then at room temperature for another month.

SMOKED CHEESES

Smoked cheeses are very popular in the north of Europe, particularly in Austria, Belgium and Germany. In essence, you can smoke any cheese, but Gouda is a good one to use, and by making it at home, you can make smoked cheese that is much better than the processed stuff you buy in the shops. American smoked cheese, however, is impossible to recreate without a factory.

Smoking works in two ways: hot-smoked and cold-smoked. Hot smoking cheese is not recommended; as the name suggests, the smoke is hot, which melts the cheese. In essence you lose texture, the fat separates and the cheese is changed irrevocably. Hot smoking is perfect, however, when you intend to cook the cheese at the same time, and one of my favourite methods involves putting some lightly grated Cheddar into an open oyster, then placing it in a hot smoker for ten minutes. Hot smokers are basically made up of a tin, which sits on a heat source, and wood, often in the form of chips, which is scattered on the bottom of the tin. The whole vessel heats up, and as the wood chars, the food is smoked and at the same time, cooked by the hot vessel. Hot smoking belongs to the realm of cooking, but it is possible to cold smoke cheese, too.

Most bought smoked cheeses are made by the addition of flavouring; real smoked cheese, in contrast is made using a smokehouse or cold-smoking machine. Smoke is produced by burning wood almost in the absence of oxygen, and the smoke is then channelled to the cheese via a pipe. The distance it travels is enough to cool the smoke so that when it touches the cheese, there is little heat to change or cook it.

You can make your own smoker by burying a fireproof receptacle in the earth and linking a long tube – say five metres; often a drainpipe is good enough – to another chamber where the cheese is smoked. Some people use a shed with a commercial smoke producer for which you buy briquettes of wood. This delivers cool smoke at the end of a tube. Another very successful smoker for cheese consists of an old fridge with a hole cut in one side for the smoke to flow into.

Which wood?

The question of which wood to use for smoking is a very personal one. I believe that resinous woods (pine and such) aren't suitable, although I did once taste a soft goats cheese smoked in pine that was unusual but quite nice. For most cheeses, though, apple is especially good: it isn't overpowering and it doesn't darken the cheese. Oak for Cheddar is also good.

Pellicle

In order to make the smoky taste adhere to the cheese you need to create a pellicle. This is an outer skin, sometimes produced by drying the cheese. More often it is made by dipping the cheese in brine and then letting it stand to dry in air. Tiny salt crystals appear on the cheese surface and act as centres for the smoke particles to grab on to.

How long to smoke?

You should always aim to smoke cheese at a temperature no higher than 22°C. The smoking time should also be slow. Large cheeses of 2kg and over (by which I mean larger than those made in the recipes in this book) should be smoked for at least 24 hours. Smaller cheeses of 500g (our recipes), should be smoked for no more than eight hours.

You have to experiment to get just what you need, bearing in mind that it will be better to smoke your cheeses lightly at first and build up from there. Unfortunately you cannot simply smoke a cheese, pull it out, taste it and put it back for some more. You really need to let it rest after smoking to allow the flavour – and preserving power – to reach the centre of the cheese. Remember that the smoking process will decrease the moisture of the cheese, and with this in mind, it's a good process to use for cheeses that are a little moist. Remember, however, that not all cheese are suitable for smoking (Brie, for example, would not work too well). Stick to the hard cheeses and only smoke lightly. A little goes a long way.

SOUTHERN EUROPEAN CHEESES

The cheeses of Spain and Italy, and to a lesser extent, France, are rarely really hard, except for Parmesan and its allies. These countries are known more for making cheeses used in cooking than for those suitable for eating with a biscuit or bread – or better still, 'stealing' between meals!

Gorgonzola

Originally from Milan, this cheese has been around since the early Middle Ages. Once plain, during one of the numerous medieval wars, it was stored incorrectly and became infected with green mould. Gorgonzola can be made from either cows or ewes milk (I prefer the latter), with salting taking place during the final stages.

5 litres milk
1 litre fresh double cream
100ml mesophillic starter
1g (⅛ teaspoon) *Penicillium roqueforti*
6 drops rennet, mixed in 1–2 tablespoons cool, boiled water
Salt to taste

1. Pour the milk and cream into a pan and warm it to 28°C. Add the starter and the *Penicillium roqueforti* and stir well.

2. Leave for 30 minutes at room temperature, then add the rennet. Leave for 1 hour, then cut the curds into 1cm cubes. Allow the curds to settle for 15 minutes or so before you carefully pour off the whey.

3. Ladle the curds into a cheesecloth-lined mould and leave them to drain for 8 hours, when the cheese will have formed. Turn it carefully out of the mould, invert it and leave it for another 8 hours.

4. Salt all surfaces by lightly rubbing the surface with a large pinch of salt and leave to stand for 2 days, salting the surfaces every time you turn them; salt and turn daily.

5. Pierce the cheese with a sterile needle so that oxygen will make the mould develop. Age it for 1 month before eating.

Feta Cheese

The EU government spoiled the interesting range of feta cheeses, which used to come from all over the southeastern countries of Europe: Greece, Bulgaria, Albania and even as far as Afghanistan. Each country had its own variety, made of ewes milk, or goats and ewes mixed, or sometimes just cows milk. The original Greek cheese was made from ewes milk, and now the only cheeses legally allowed to be named feta come from Greece. The interesting relationship between cheese and mankind is now a little harder to fathom, because all those other 'little fetas' have somehow lost their place in the world. As a reflection of its variations, however, this recipe is slightly different to the one for feta given on page 88.

5 litres milk
450ml buttermilk
6 drops rennet
Brine, made using 200g of salt per litre of water

1. Heat the milk to 32°C. Add the buttermilk and keep the mixture at this temperature for 1 hour. Add the rennet and stir in, leaving for 45 minutes to set.

2. Cut into 1cm cubes and leave in the whey for 20 minutes. Try to keep the cheese as near to 32°C as possible.

3. Ladle the curds and whey into a cheesecloth-lined colander and leave to drain overnight covered. The cheese will shrivel and combine into a mass.

4. Take the block out of the colander and cut it into 3 or 4 pieces. Sprinkle them with salt on all sides.

5. Leave at room temperature for 24 hours, turning the cheese pieces at least 5 or 6 times and resalting any wet areas where the whey has been drawn out by the salt.

6. Leave the pieces uncovered for a week, then cut them into 1cm cubes and store in the brine.

7. When ready to use, remove the cheese from the brine, but be prepared for it to dry quickly and shrivel. Some recipes call for feta to be stored in olive oil, not brine, which makes it a little slippy but completely divine in flavour. You can also add whole garlic cloves or jalapeño peppers to the oil.

Halloumi

Halloumi originally came from Cyprus and is a traditional goats cheese. There are no starters involved. It was one of the central cheeses included in the diet of more or less the whole of the eastern Mediterranean, North Africa and parts of Spain, where goats were the most common source of milk. There is still great debate as to whether the goat has changed the landscape of the region by eating the vegetation, or whether the landscape is suitable for goats alone. Whatever the truth of the matter, the goat is the very best animal at turning meagre rations into useful human food. Halloumi is usually stored in a little whey in jars. Consequently, it needs to be kept in a cool place, otherwise the whey will go off. These days, however, you can buy it wrapped in paper, although you can still see some of the wetness of the whey.

5 litres fresh milk (goats, ewes or cows)
8 drops rennet (yes, more than normal)
1 teaspoon salt

1. Pour the milk into a large pan and warm it to around 25°C. Add the rennet.

2. Leave for 1 hour. When the curds have formed, ladle them into a cheesecloth-lined colander.

3. Cut the curds into cubes and mix a level teaspoon of salt into them.

4. Reserve the whey in a pan as it drains. Once drained, leave the curds to stand on a cheese mat.

5. Bring the whey to the boil and add the curds. Reduce the heat and simmer until the cheese floats to the top. Remove the cheese and set aside to cool.

6. Store in jars, with a little whey added, in a cool place.

BRITISH CHEESES

This chapter contains recipes for some British cheeses that have not already been mentioned earlier, such as Cheddar and so on. The UK has a long history of making cheese; although there is very little written evidence to back it up, cheese-making here was probably pre-Roman in origin. Certainly it was the Romans who brought cheese with them to these shores, and there are many remnants of cheese-making equipment in the UK as well as accounts of Roman cheese-making here.

Roman cheese-makers used a 'rennet' taken from plant material, and preferred goats and ewes milk to cows milk. The rennet was added in the ratio of the weight of one denarius to a bucket of milk. Roman cheese was much saltier than modern cheese, due mainly to the need for cheese to travel. If, as I suppose, many modern British cheeses have their origins in the Roman occupation, this might explain the greater variety of cheese in England than in Scotland, which was never under Roman rule. In any case, cheese-making throughout these islands has become not only big business, but a craft that more or less copies the cheeses of Europe and the rest of the world.

For example, you can get a 'Stilton' from Ireland, a blue from Scotland and a 'Brie' from Wales. Cheese-making has become more cosmopolitan, with people making whatever they can rather than what they have always produced for generations. Today, there is a huge and growing interest in making cheese in the kitchen, and you can create a very close approximation of traditional British cheeses at home.

The recipes included in this chapter are only approximations, but they do work. I've made them all, although elements of the cheese-

making process cause variations in flavour. Even with large vats, temperature-controlled processes and perfect maturing conditions, cheeses vary from batch to batch. So how difficult is it to create a similar amount of uniformity in the kitchen? Again, if you do nothing else, stick to the temperatures and the processes associated with them. In cheese-making, temperature is everything.

What's in a name?

How, you may ask, can you call a homemade Caerphilly-type cheese a Caerphilly and not just a '13 Wimbledon Terrace' cheese? Well, the recipes in this chapter create something of the characteristics of the original cheese model – usually acidity and creaminess – as well as consistency. It isn't possible in the kitchen to recreate some of the very high pressures used in modern cheese manufacture, yet these recipes often produce cheeses that are more true to the original type in texture and consistency than anything you could buy in the shops.

Why size matters

Another important consideration is how much cheese you can make and mature at any given time. It is one thing to make a huge block of cheese from many gallons of milk in a large vat and mature it for three months in a clean room; it is quite another to make 500g of cheese from 4.5 litres of milk and mature it without growing all kinds of fungi and bacteria. Consequently, be sure the container in which you store your cheese is sterile. And, if any mould growths appear that are not naturally associated with the cheese, discard it straight away.

Caerphilly Cheese

A spell-checker produced this joke, but it's true nonetheless: you have to make Caerphilly carefully. This cheese has its origin in the southwest of England, southeast of Wales. Traditionally it was salty; some say it was miners' cheese and that the extra saltiness was put there on purpose to add salt to miners' diets. I used to let it mature for a month, because the salting keeps the cheese fresh. However, I went through a period of not resisting this cheese, so it lasted only a fortnight in the maturing box in the fridge.

5 litres milk
1 sachet mesophillic starter
5 drops rennet, mixed in 1–2 tablespoons cooled, boiled water
Salt
Brine, made by adding 300g salt per litre of water

1. Pour the milk in a pan and gently heat or keep it warm so that it reaches 20°C.

2. Add the starter, stir and heat the mixture to 34°C. Wait for 45 minutes before adding the rennet. Stir it in well.

3. Leave the milk to set until the curd forms; this can take up to 1 hour.

4. When the curd forms, cut it into 1cm cubes and gently stir for 15 minutes. This will remove some of the whey.

5. Allow the curd to settle for 15 minutes, then gently heat it, raising the temperature over 1 hour to 34°C, stirring constantly.

6. Pour the curds into a cheesecloth-lined colander and leave to drain, then sprinkle a level teaspoon and a half of salt evenly over them. Transfer the curds in the cheesecloth to a mould and apply light pressure (5kg) overnight to drain the whey.

7. Open up the cheesecloth and allow the curds to fall apart, then float the curds in brine. Float for 24 hours, then return the curds to the sterile mould and press lightly overnight (5kg).

Cheshire Cheese

When I was a child, my grandmother used to make this cheese and I ate it with strong pickled shallots. I think it is this that started my personal journey with dairy products. Over the years I have varied the recipe to suit my own tastes, but the following is an easy version to make. Traditionally, Cheshire is dipped in lard, which is something I never used to do because I never made cheeses big enough to require it. However, lard (rather than wax) does work well on such a delicate cheese. You can use 125ml natural, unflavoured yoghurt instead of mesophillic starter if you prefer.

5 litres milk
1 sachet mesophillic starter
5 drops rennet, mixed in 1 tablespoon cooled, boiled water
Salt

1. Pour the milk into a large pan, add the starter and slowly warm to 29°C. Leave the mixture at this temperature for 45 minutes.

2. Add the rennet and leave for another 60 minutes to form the curd.

3. Cut the curds into 1cm cubes. Over about 30 minutes, increase the temperature to 35°C, then allow the curds to settle for 30 minutes.

4. Ladle the whey out of the pan and cut the curds into 10cm squares; pile them at the back of the pan. Draw off all the whey and allow the curds to drain in this position. Move the position of the blocks every 30 minutes for a total of 90 minutes.

5. Once drained, break up the curds into 1cm pieces and add salt to taste (the usual measure is 1% salt per weight of curds).

6. Place into a cheesecloth-lined mould and press lightly overnight – use no more than 5kg.

7. The following day, double the weight and press at this level for 2 more days, taking the cheese out, turning it over and replacing it in the mould each morning and afternoon.

8. Brush the cheese with melted lard, or simply dip it. Leave in a sterile container in the fridge for a fortnight to mature.

Colwick Cheese

This is the nearest you can get to British peasant's cheese. It was made in the village of Colwick, in Nottinghamshire (so quite possibly was eaten by Robin Hood). This recipe uses nothing but milk, and if you can collect as many different dregs of milk that are going off, all the better. Add a cup of yoghurt to make it creamier, and it will also improve the setting time. Traditionally it was served in the middle of a dish that was filled with fruit. Sometimes sugar was added and the result was shared by two people, which gave it the name 'lover's cheese'.

Milk: as much as you want!

1. Keep the milk at room temperature for up to 1 week (milk straight from the cow will take only a couple of days). Once the acidity increases enough to curdle it, leave it for another couple of hours and the curds will be fully set.

2. Pour the curds into a muslin bag and allow them to drain. (My granny used to hang it on the washing line and the grass was scorched beneath.)

3. When it has stopped dripping, dip the bag under running water to completely remove the whey that remains, washing away any smell.

4. This cheese can be used as is, or you can add cream or herbs. You can give it a light pressing in a mould if you like, or simply spoon it into a dish and leave it.

Creamy Lancashire Cheese

This is a bit like Cheshire, but creamier, with a flakiness that is absolutely lovely. It isn't a Cheddar because it isn't pressed as heavily and isn't cheddared – i.e. stacking the curds so they drain over each other. The buttermilk starter is great, and I add cream, too. The resulting cheese is so rich that it's like eating Cornish ice cream, only it's salty and not sweet, and it's warm, not cold. So actually nothing like ice cream, really, but you know what I mean!

400ml buttermilk
400ml cream
5 litres milk
6 drops rennet, mixed in 1–2 tablespoons cooled, boiled water
1 level teaspoon salt

1. In a large pan, add the buttermilk and the cream to the milk and warm it slowly until it reaches 30°C. (I put a lid on the pan, remove it from the heat and wrap the whole thing in towels so that it stays warm – but do not put towels near the cooker!)

2. Add the rennet and stir well, then leave it until the curd sets.

3. When the curd forms, cut it into 1cm cubes, stir gently for 15 minutes, then allow the curds to settle for 30 minutes.

4. Pour the curds into a muslin-lined colander and allow them to drain. Once they've stopped draining, add the salt and continue to drain. The salt brings out more whey.

5. Spoon the cheese into a muslin-lined mould, and press it for 48 hours with about 10kg of pressure (or a 10kg weight).

6. You can wax or bandage the cheese (see page 55) and it should be completely wonderful in a month. Or simply leave it in a sterile container for a couple of weeks before eating.

Wensleydale Cheese

This is Yorkshire Cheese, made originally by the monks of North Yorkshire and sold in villages all over the county. Some say that, today, Wensleydale is no longer made in Yorkshire, but this isn't the case: try telling that to the myriad producers in farmhouses all over the Ridings. Initially Wensleydale was a ewes milk cheese – which makes perfect sense, given that the great monasteries built up incredible wealth from wool and sheep. For the last couple of centuries, however, the cheese has been made from cows milk. This recipe calls for creamy milk, so if you know anyone who has a Jersey, then this is the cheese for you. Ewes milk is very creamy and, of course, perfect for this job. If you want white cheese, don't add the Penicillium roqueforti. I almost always do add it, however. I used to wax this cheese, but don't bother these days; the mould needs oxygen to work, so I simply leave it in a sterile container, opening the lid every day to freshen the air.

5 litres really creamy milk
1g (⅛ teaspoon) *Penicillium roqueforti*
100ml mesophillic starter
5 drops rennet, mixed in 1–2 tablespoons cooled, boiled water
1 level teaspoon salt

1. In a large pan, heat the milk to 30°C. Stir in the *Penicillium roqueforti* and starter and keep the mixture at the same temperature for 45–60 minutes.

2. Add the rennet and leave the mixture for 1 hour to set.

3. Cut the curds into large cubes and allow to rest for 30 minutes. During that time, slowly raise the temperature to 35°C.

4. Pour into a cheesecloth-lined colander and drain for 20 minutes.

5. Re-cut the curds into 1cm cubes and drain off any remaining whey.

6. Sprinkle with the salt, which will draw out more whey.

7. Put the curds into a muslin-lined mould and press lightly (5kg) overnight.

8. Bandage or wax the cheese (see page 55) and ripen it for 1 month before using.

MANUFACTURED CHEESES

You don't need a factory to make the cheeses in this chapter. What I mean by 'manufactured cheeses' is those with a need for extra processing. There is either a treatment (chemical or heating) or a technique (such as kneading) required to make or approximate these recipes. The ricotta on page 114, , for example, has to be re-cooked – no surprise there, though, as the word *ricotta* itself means 'to cook again'.

A number of industrial processes are used to make ricotta, but all of them are associated with boiling the protein in milk, known as albumin, in order to precipitate it. It is a bit like boiling an egg to set the white, and in fact, the proteins involved are similar.

Mozzarella

Mozzarella is one of those cheeses that has taken over the world. A generation ago, most people in the UK didn't really know it existed, let alone bought it. Today, of course, it's available in supermarkets in little plastic bags with added brine to prevent it from drying out. Mozzarella is 'plasticised', which means that it is kneaded; the process makes it springy and stringy – just that pizza consistency everyone enjoys. The word 'mozzarella' comes from the manufacturing process. It is kneaded and spun, then cut into short strands ('mozza' means 'to cut' in Italian). The cheese originated in Italy, and there are about seven or eight types, only one of which is made from buffalo milk (the others are made from cows milk). Note: You'll need to start this recipe in the evening.

5 litres milk
75ml plain natural yoghurt
75ml buttermilk
6 drops rennet, mixed in 1–2 tablespoons cooled, boiled water
Brine, made by using 200g salt per litre of water

1. Heat the milk to 32°C and keep it at this temperature. Add the yoghurt and buttermilk and stir vigorously to remove any lumps. Leave for 45 minutes.

2. Add the rennet and mix well. Wait 1 hour, then cut the curds into 1cm cubes, all the while keeping the temperature constant.

3. Stir gently with a clean hand and allow the curds to settle for 15 minutes, then gently drain them into a muslin-lined colander. They will form a single mass quite easily, which you should then wash in cold water. Let them drain in the refrigerator overnight.

4. The next day, allow the curds to warm to room temperature. The culture will still be growing and the acidity of the curds will increase. Cut all the cheese into small cubes and put them into a pan covered with water at 72°C. Allow the temperature to drop to around 55°C and squeeze the cubes together. Knead by joining and stretching.

5. Form balls of cheese that weigh around 250g each (you should get 2 from 5 litres of milk). Salt them for 12 hours in brine, and your mozzarella will be ready to use.

Processed Cheese

Often called 'sweepings up', which means that the cheese is made from discarded pieces of cheese in the factory. Actually, processed cheese is made under pressure, melted in such a way as to reconstitute it with little loss in fat content. The cheese is then heat-treated, emulsifying salts are added and the lot is heated to over 100°C in a vast pressure cooker. If the cheese is to be squeezed out of a tube, some water is added; otherwise it is extruded into sheets or whatever is needed. The point of this cheese is that it doesn't separate into fat and solids on heating, but remains stable. The only problem is that I think it tastes awful! That said, you can make an approximate processed cheese by using almost any bits of cheeses you may have left over in the following manner.

1. Cut the 'leftovers' into small pieces and put them in a pan with a little milk equal to about 10% of the amount of cheese. It is important that the cheese isn't handled too much to avoid spurious bacteria.

2. Heat this very slowly, and as the cheese melts, stir constantly so that all the solids and as much fat as possible mix. This is best done in a bain marie, or water bath.

3. As soon as all the cheese has melted, turn off the heat. Continue stirring all the time, making sure that, as the cheese mass cools, it doesn't separate.

4. Eventually the cheese will start to solidify again, and you can then pour the mass into moulds to set.

Ricotta

This ricotta is basically acidified milk that is heated to a high but carefully controlled temperature and the result is a cheese made up of two types of curds. Casein curds form because of the acid and albuminous curds form because of the temperature. The two are then collected. Be careful not to lose the curds through the cheesecloth. Some people add garlic and olive oil to ricotta and it is frequently used in ravioli recipes.

5 litres full-fat milk
Juice of 4 lemons
Salt

1. In a large pan, combine the milk and lemon juice.

2. Slowly heat the milk, being careful not to scald it on the sides of the pan. (You can use a water bath for this part of the process.)

3. At 83°C, the curds will rise to the surface. Leave the milk at this temperature for 15 minutes. Meanwhile, dampen and fold cheesecloths into 5–6 layers. Use only the finest grade material.

4. Carefully ladle the curds onto the cheesecloths and pull the corners together to hang. Drain in the fridge, if possible, for 4 hours.

5. Carefully salt to 1% by weight (see page 106) and store in the fridge.

Raclette

Raclette is a kind of Swiss fondue which is made by holding the cheese in front of the fire and allowing it to melt, then scraping the melted cheese away (the word 'raclette' means 'to scrape'). So this recipe makes a good melting cheese. You really do need a double boiler in order to warm the cheese slowly enough: the process must be done slowly and gently. Use this basic raclette in a fondue kit, or if you're lucky enough to have a fire, put a metal pan set beside it, dip bread into it and enjoy!

5 litres fresh full-fat milk
100ml mesophillic starter
6 drops rennet, mixed in 1–2 tablespoons cooled, boiled water
1 level teaspoon salt
Brine, made of 330g salt per litre of water

1. Warm the milk to 32°C. Add the starter, mixing well, and leave it to work for 1 hour.

2. Add the rennet and stir constantly with a whisk for 5 minutes.

3. Allow the cheese to set for 1 hour, then cut the curds into 5mm cubes. Leave them to sit for 30 minutes.

4. Boil a kettle of water and allow it to cool to 50°C. Set aside to wash the curds.

5. Give the curds a stir and ladle away a measured amount of whey, replacing it with the same amount of cooled, boiled water. Repeat until all the washing water has been used up; the process takes around an hour.

6. Allow the curds to rest for an hour, slowly removing the whey as you go.

7. Add the salt, then drain the curds into a cheesecloth-lined colander.

8. Shape the cheese in the cloth and place it into the brine. After 6 hours, turn the cheese over and give it another 6 hours in brine. Repeat this step once more, then remove and leave the cheese to dry on a cheese mat until ready to use.

COOKING
WITH CHEESE

With a name like *Making Your Own Cheese,* this book is obviously dedicated to the creation of cheese in all its many varieties, but in this chapter you'll also learn how to cook with it.

Cheese is a food that can be eaten with pleasure with very few other ingredients: a simple plate of crackers and pickles, maybe a little salad and, of course, your favourite cheese, makes a satisfying and speedy lunch. But being a little more adventurous can bring amazing dishes to the table using this wonderful foodstuff – which is precisely why my wife, Diana, and I have included the recipes here that will help expand your enjoyment.

SNACKS AND STARTERS

Pizza Toasties

This is a great way to show off two types of your cheese. Add other ingredients such as tuna, chopped chorizo sausage or prawns if you wish.

SERVES 2

4 slices bread
3 tablespoons tomato purée
1 tablespoon olive oil
1 garlic clove, grated or crushed
1 tablespoon water
50g mozzarella-type cheese, cut into slices
50g Cheddar-type cheese, grated or chopped
12 black olives
8 anchovy fillets
Black pepper

1. Lightly toast the bread.

2. Mix the tomato purée, olive oil, garlic and water together in a small bowl. Spread evenly over the slices of toast.

3. Top with the slices of mozzarella and Cheddar.

4. Place the olives and anchovies on top of the cheese and sprinkle with black pepper.

5. Place on a baking sheet and cook at the hottest part of the oven at 225°C/gas mark 7 until the cheese begins to bubble. Serve immediately.

Rarebits

*Slices of cheese toasted on bread is always a favourite, but try these
simple variations for a change.*

SERVES 2

Mix 100g grated Cheddar-type cheese with 1 teaspoon Dijon mustard
and 2 tablespoons light ale

•

Mix 100g grated crumbly cheese with 1 teaspoon wholegrain mustard
and 2 tablespoons Guinness

•

Mix 50g grated Cheddar-type cheese with 2 tablespoons cottage
cheese and ½ tablespoon chopped chives

•

Mix 100g grated cheese (any firmer cheese will do) and
2 tablespoons red onion chutney

1. Use any of these combinations to top hot, buttered toast. Simply grill for a few minutes
until bubbling.

Potted Cheese

This makes an excellent snack or starter course served with thin slices of toasted bread.
These can be made and kept in the fridge for 2–3 days. As a variation, add 25g chopped
smoked salmon to the cheese mixture and a tablespoon of chopped dill or parsley (this should
be consumed within 24 hours, though).

SERVES 4

220g any firm cheese, grated
1 tablespoon chopped fresh herbs
100g softened butter
20g melted butter

1. Mix the cheese, herbs and softened butter together and press into 4 ramekin dishes.

2. Pour a small amount of melted butter over the top to 'seal' the potted cheese, cover and place in the fridge to set.

French Beans with Cheshire Cheese

This lovely dish can be served as a light lunch or a starter.

SERVES 3–4

500g French beans
2 garlic cloves
1 tablespoon olive or sunflower oil
80g Cheshire-type cheese
½ teaspoon paprika
2 tomatoes, thinly sliced

1. Wash, top and tail the beans and cook them in lightly salted, boiling water for 5 minutes. Drain and refresh in cold water to stop them from going too soft.

2. Butter or oil an ovenproof dish, cut the garlic cloves in half and rub them all over the sides of the dish. This will give a hint of garlic flavour to the dish. If you prefer a stronger garlic taste, then chop the cloves and mix them with the beans.

3. Preheat the oven to 190°C/gas mark 5. Place the beans in the dish evenly and drizzle with the oil.

4. Crumble or slice the cheese and lay it on top of the beans.

5. Sprinkle with the paprika and lay the tomatoes on the top.

6. Cook in the hottest part of the oven for 15–20 minutes, then serve with garlic bread.

Broccoli Cheese Pasties

A fun way of eating broccoli: children love them!

SERVES 4

20g butter
20g plain flour
400ml milk
½ teaspoon dry mustard
100g strong Cheddar-type cheese, grated
1 broccoli head, broken into 16 small spears
Salt and pepper to taste
1 small egg, beaten
1 tablespoon grated Parmesan-type cheese
300g puff pastry

1. Make the cheese sauce by melting the butter in a pan and stirring in the flour over a low heat. Add a little of the milk at a time, stirring it into the roux; when all the milk has been incorporated, turn up the heat to medium, bring slowly to the boil and cook for 2 minutes. Remove from the heat.

2. Stir in the mustard and Cheddar cheese, and leave to one side. Steam or boil the broccoli until tender. Drain.

3. Roll out the pastry until quite thin to about 4mm in thickness. Cut into 8 equal squares measuring about 10cm by 10cm. Stir the broccoli into the cheese sauce.

4. Place an equal spoonful into the centre of each pastry square and dampen the edges. Bring the edges together to form a round pasty shape. Place on a greased baking sheet and preheat the oven to 200°C/gas mark 6.

5. Brush the tops of the pasties and sprinkle with Parmesan. Make a slit in the top of each pasty and bake for about 20 minutes until well-risen and golden in colour.

6. Cool slightly, then serve hot or cold with a green salad and fresh tomatoes.

Twice-baked Cheese Soufflés

These make an excellent starter course and are easy to make, unlike a normal soufflé which can be very nerve-racking indeed!

SERVES 4

280ml milk
1 small, peeled shallot (or a slice of onion)
Salt and pepper to taste
50g each butter and plain flour
½ level teaspoon dry mustard
200g firm Cheddar-type cheese, grated
4 eggs, separated
350ml single cream • Ground paprika, for dusting

1. Preheat the oven to 180°C/gas mark 4. Butter 4 ramekins. Put the milk, shallot and salt and pepper in a sturdy pan and bring to simmering. Strain and reserve the milk; discard the onion.

2. Melt the butter in a saucepan over a low heat. Add the flour and mustard and mix with a wooden spoon. Cook for a few seconds, then stir in the hot milk gradually.

3. Add 150g of the cheese and the egg yolks. Check the seasoning and adjust if necessary. Remove from the heat.

4. Whisk the egg whites until stiff and fold them into the cheese sauce mixture.

5. Fill the ramekins ¾ of way full with the mixture and stand them in a roasting pan. Pour boiling water into the pan until it reaches a quarter of the way up the sides of the ramekins. Bake for about 15 minutes until they are well-risen and set. Remove from the oven and allow to sink and go cool.

6. Heat the oven to 220°C/gas mark 7. Butter a shallow ovenproof dish. Remove the soufflés from the ramekins and place them in the dish.

7. Season the cream and pour it over the soufflés. Sprinkle with the remaining cheese and paprika. Bake for 10-12 minutes until they begin to brown, and serve immediately with a green salad.

Stilton and Leek Soup

Don't be tempted to add salt to this soup as you prepare it, because the cheese is already salty. Try it after adding the cheese and season then if you need to.

SERVES 4

50g butter
2–3 leeks, depending on size, cut into discs
1 litre water
2 medium potatoes, peeled and cut into small chunks
2 bay leaves
Black pepper to taste
220g Stilton-type cheese, crumbled
3 tablespoons crème fraîche or single cream

1. Melt the butter in a pan and add the leeks. Cook over a very low heat for 10–15 minutes, until soft but not brown.

2. Add the water, potatoes and bay leaves. Season with black pepper.

3. Bring to the boil, then reduce the heat and simmer for 25–30 minutes.

4. Remove the bay leaves.

5. Add the cheese and stir over a low heat for 5 minutes.

6. For a smooth soup, either transfer to a blender or use a hand blender to whizz it until it is as smooth as you require.

7. Reheat before serving and swirl in a little crème fraîche or cream.

SALADS

Many a wonderful salad can be prepared in a flash using all different kinds of cheese. Here are some of my favourites.

Goats Cheese with Chicory and Apple

Do try to use the walnut oil in this recipe: it makes a difference to the flavour of the salad.

Serves 2

8 chicory leaves
1 red and 1 green apple
2 celery sticks, chopped
50g walnuts, chopped
3 tablespoons lemon juice
2 tablespoons walnut oil
2 goats cheese rounds, each weighing about 25g

1. Cut the apples into thin slices, removing the core. Drizzle with 1 tablespoon of the lemon juice.

2. Arrange the leaves on 2 plates and arrange the apple slices evenly over them.

3. Sprinkle with the celery and walnuts.

4. Combine the rest of the lemon juice and walnut oil and drizzle over the salad.

5. Brown the goats cheese on one side under a very hot grill and place in the centre of the each salad. Serve immediately.

Watercress with Camembert Fritters

I love deep-fried cheese, but you must make sure the oil has reached 190°C so that, as it crisps on the outside, the inside remains firm.

SERVES 2

100g fresh breadcrumbs
Oil for frying
1 small Camembert, cut into 8 wedges
1 egg
6cm piece cucumber
2 large handfuls watercress
4 spring onions, trimmed and sliced in half
2 dessertspoons cranberry jelly

1. Toast the breadcrumbs in the oven for 5 minutes at 190°C/gas mark 5.

2. Heat the oil until it reaches the correct temperature. Dip the cheese wedges into the egg, then into the breadcrumbs. Fry until just golden brown and leave to drain on kitchen paper.

3. Chop the cucumber into small dice.

4. Arrange the watercress on 2 plates and spread the cucumber evenly over the leaves.

5. Arrange the spring onions around the plates.

6. Add the spoonful of cranberry jelly to the side of each plate and place the hot cheese on top. Serve immediately.

Mozzarella and Avocado Salad

This is an excellent way to show off your homemade mozzarella-style cheese.

SERVES 4 AS A MAIN MEAL, 6 AS A STARTER

2 large beef tomatoes, each cut into 6 thin slices
2 ripe avocados, peeled and cut into thin slices
150g mozzarella-type cheese, cut into 12 slices
2 large spring onions, chopped finely

For the dressing
3 tablespoons white-wine vinegar
2 tablespoons extra-virgin olive oil
1 tablespoon runny honey
1 tablespoon chopped chives
Salt and pepper to taste

1. Whisk all the dressing ingredients together and season with salt and pepper to taste.

2. Arrange the tomatoes, avocado and cheese alternately on single plates.

3. Sprinkle over the chopped onions.

4. Drizzle the dressing over so all the ingredients are equally covered. Serve immediately.

MAIN MEALS

Cheese Rice

This unusual dish was developed from a popular Victorian recipe. It can be served with salad or a green vegetable. Beware: it is very filling, so go easy on any other carbohydrate. As a variation, line the buttered dish with slices of tomato and lay the rice mixture on top.

SERVES 2–3

120g rice
80g Cheddar-type cheese, grated
30g Parmesan-type cheese, grated
280ml milk
15g butter
4 tablespoons single cream
Cayenne pepper
Salt to taste

1. Butter a pie dish.

2. Boil the rice in sufficient water to cover with about 2.5cm to spare. Drain when cooked.

3. Warm the milk in a pan and stir in the Cheddar-type cheese, butter and cream. When the butter and cheese have melted, add the rice and stir well. Season with salt to taste.

4. Fill the pie dish with the mixture and dust the top with a little cayenne pepper. Sprinkle the Parmesan-type cheese on top.

5. Bake for 20–30 minutes at 190°C/gas mark 5. Serve immediately.

Baked Cheese-topped Onions

These make a wonderful winter supper dish, or can be served with grilled pork steak or sausages.

SERVES 2

2 medium onions, peeled and halved
(round the centre, not from root to tip)
½ teaspoon dried or 1 teaspoon fresh thyme
Salt and pepper
2 tablespoons sunflower, olive or rapeseed oil
150g red Leicester-type cheese, sliced

1. Preheat the oven to 190°C/gas mark 5.

2. Place the halved onions on a baking tray and drizzle them with oil. Sprinkle evenly with the thyme and season with salt and pepper.

3. Bake for 20–25 minutes or until they are beginning to brown.

4. Place slices of the cheese on top of the onions and put back in the oven for 10 more minutes, or until the cheese has melted. Serve immediately.

Cheese and Vegetable Layer Pie

Quite a spectacular dish that is ideal to serve at a dinner party. Use any other cooked vegetables: a layer of mushrooms, broad beans or sliced leeks. Be creative and remember to think about the colour scheme of your layers.

SERVES 6

1 litre thick béchamel sauce
200g fresh spinach leaves
1kg mixture of freshly cooked carrots, cauliflower, broccoli, baby
sweetcorn and green beans; well-drained and separated
150g Cheddar- or similar-type cheese
3 ripe tomatoes, skins removed and sliced
3 tablespoons fresh breadcrumbs
3 tablespoons grated Parmesan-type cheese
Salt and black pepper
½ teaspoon paprika

1. Butter a deep casserole dish: a clear one is best because you see the layers clearly and it looks amazing. Divide the white sauce into three equal parts.

2. Cook the spinach in a little water until just wilted. Squeeze out the water and stir into one part of the white sauce, blend to mix or liquidise.

3. Add the grated Cheddar-type cheese to another section of the sauce and season the third with the paprika.

4. Preheat the oven to 200°C/gas mark 6. Start to layer the contents, firstly with the carrots and cauliflower, then the paprika sauce. Then the broccoli, tomatoes and the green sauce. Finally, add the sweetcorn, the green beans and the cheese sauce. Finish with the breadcrumbs and grated Parmesan-type cheese.

5. Bake for 20–25 minutes, or until the topping begins to brown. Serve with boiled new or baked potatoes.

Lamb and Feta Burgers

These burgers have a little secret in the centre: they contain feta cheese. Great for barbecues or just when you fancy an unusual burger. These are delicious served in a burger bun, and we like them with couscous flavoured with a little chopped mint and lemon juice.

SERVES 4

500g lamb mince
1 level teaspoon ground cumin
½ teaspoon dried or 1 teaspoon chopped fresh mint
1 level teaspoon salt, black pepper to taste
100g feta-type cheese, cut into 8 cubes

1. Combine the lamb, cumin, mint, salt and black pepper with your hands and form into 8 equal patties.

2. Place a cube of cheese in the centre of each one and bring the sides up to cover the cheese. Flatten down slightly, being careful to keep the cheese hidden in the meat.

3. Either fry in a little oil on both sides for about 4 minutes each side, or cook them on your barbecue.

CAKES AND DESSERTS

Golden Ricotta Cake

A moist cake that keeps well in a container in the fridge – but it tastes so good it will be eaten up in a flash!

SERVES 8

180g butter, at room temperature
1 tablespoon golden syrup
150g muscovado sugar
150g self-raising flour
3 eggs, well-beaten
250g ricotta cheese
Grated zest and juice of 1 lemon
30g ground almonds

1. Preheat the oven to 180°C/gas mark 4. Butter and line an 18cm springform cake tin.

2. Cream the butter, sugar and syrup together until light and fluffy.

3. Add 1 tablespoon of the flour and the eggs, ricotta and lemon juice and zest. Beat well.

4. Fold in the flour and the almonds.

5. Spoon the mixture into the tin and level out the top.

6. Turn down the heat to 170°C/gas mark 3 as soon as you put the tin in the oven and bake for 35–40 minutes.

7. Leave to cool in the tin.

Curd Cheesecake

This is like the delicious Yorkshire curd tarts I had when I was a student living in Leeds.

SERVES 4

200g shortcrust pastry
200g curd cheese
25g melted butter
1 large egg, beaten
1 tablespoon golden caster sugar
1 tablespoon golden syrup
30g currants
Juice and zest of 1 lemon

1. Preheat the oven to 200°C/gas mark 6. Grease an 18cm flan or pie dish.

2. Roll out the pastry and use it to line the pie dish.

3. Put the curd cheese, butter, egg, sugar, syrup, currants and lemon zest and juice in a bowl and combine well with a wooden spoon.

4. Spoon the filling into the pastry case and smooth out the top.

5. Bake for 25–30 minutes, or until it has turned light golden in colour. Cool before serving.

Cream Cheese Ice Cream

This rich-tasting ice cream goes really well with fresh summer fruits or as a topping for a slice of hot apple pie. It is a very rich and creamy ice cream, so keep the portions small.

250g cream cheese, beaten with a wooden spoon
100ml sour cream
100ml single cream
150g white caster sugar
Juice of 1 lemon

1. Put all the ingredients together in a food processor and blend until light and smooth.

2. Transfer to a lidded freezable container and leave to freeze completely.

3. Just before serving, remove from the freezer for 5 minutes.

A WORD ABOUT CHEESEBOARDS

After a meal or as part of a buffet party, a good-quality cheeseboard is always a winner, and here are a few ways you can make the most of it. Try serving a small variety of cheese cut in large slices rather than lots of little pieces; three different types is often the best for balance. Think about colour, texture and strength of flavour when choosing the cheeses.

Remove the cheese from the fridge about 30 minutes before serving to allow it to come to room temperature – unless it is very hot weather, then 10 minutes will probably be sufficient. This allows the flavours to develop.

Serve with fresh crackers or biscuits, or bread and some butter. Fruit makes an excellent accompaniment to cheese: all colours of grapes, figs, apples and pears. Celery sticks (put them in a glass with a little ice-cold water to keep fresh) also go really well. Leave the inner, yellowy leaves on the stalks to add colour.

It is important not to squash different cheeses onto the board, so leave sufficient room between them so that they may be easily cut.

CHEESES
FOR SWEETS

It was a serious eye-opener to me to learn that you could have sweet cheese. It just didn't seem right – until one day I realised that rice pudding was made from sweetened milk, and therefore, somehow, sweet cheese would be just as good. It was many years before I left home and sampled the delights of cheesecake and tiramisu, something my mother's generation would never have dreamed of.

Some of the cheeses in this chapter are made using lemon juice as a coagulant and, once sweetened, are super for cheesecakes because they retain the lemon flavour. Whether to omit salt in a cheese destined for a sweet dish has long been a cause for debate. In my opinion, however, salt is important, not only as a preservative, but mostly as a way of driving whey out of the curds, and to omit it would be a mistake.

You can sweeten any of these cheeses with sugar or honey, but I think cheese is best sweetened by adding other naturally sweet foods, such as fruit. The affinity of apples for salt makes this combination a traditional partnership, but strawberries, pineapple and gooseberries work well, too, as do raisins.

Paneer

Paneer is a rubbery cheese, similar in texture to tofu. Although it is fairly bland on its own, it makes a great ingredient in other dishes because it readily absorbs flavours. In desserts it gives a creamy freshness to dishes.

3 litres full-fat milk
200ml natural yoghurt
3–4 tablespoons white vinegar

1. Pour the milk into a large pan and very slowly increase the temperature until it boils. Keep stirring the milk so that it doesn't stick, as this alters its flavour.

2. As soon as the milk begins to boil, lower the heat and add the yoghurt and white vinegar, stirring gently so that the vinegar is completely mixed in. The curds should appear very quickly and when they do, remove the pan from the heat completely.

3. Over the next 15 minutes, leave the pan to stand undisturbed so that the curds harden and the vinegar has time to work.

4. Line a colander with muslin or cheesecloth and pour in the curds to drain off the whey. After approximately 10 minutes, gather the corners of the cloth and tie it up, twisting gently (if required) to drain off any further whey. Run the bag of curds under a cold tap until you have removed the vinegar taste.

5. Lay the bundle on a chopping board or a flat tray and place something heavy (saucepan full of water) on it, ensuring that the pressure is even and fully covers the bundle. This will allow any further whey to escape, and helps hardens the curds.

6. For best results, leave the curds – now paneer – to set for 3–4 hours. Once set. remove the saucepan and then slowly remove the cloth. The slab of paneer is now ready to cut into cubes.

7. If you wish, fry the cubes lightly in oil until brown on all sides. They are now ready to be added to your chosen curries, or even to salads and sweets. Alternatively, salt them and leave them in brine, or sweeten them to use in cheesecake, etc.

Neufchâtel

This is a French cheese from Normandy and was originally made from goats milk. It can be made from any milk, however, and is a great substitute for cream cheese. This version uses whole milk, not cream. I have added this cheese to the sweets section because it is the best goats cheese to eat with fruit. I don't really like goats cheese, so if I like this, it really must be good!

5 litres fresh full-fat milk
100ml mesophillic starter
8 drops rennet, mixed in 1–2 tablespoons cool, boiled water
Salt to taste

1. Combine the milk with the starter and leave the mixture for an hour at room temperature.

2. Add the rennet to the milk, cover and set aside to set overnight at 20°C; wrap the pan in a couple of towels to keep the temperature up.

3. Line a colander with a fine cheesecloth and ladle in the curds. Drain for around 8 hours, then draw up the corners of the cloth and hang it up to drain further.

4. Mix the curds by hand until they become a little like pasta. Drain again and and place them in a bowl.

5. Season with a teaspoon or so of salt.

Queso Blanco

Queso blanco ('white cheese'), from South America, uses lemon juice to set the curds.

5 litres full-fat milk
Juice of 4 lemons
Salt

1. Heat the milk until it is at 82°C. Stir constantly to prevent burning and maintain the temperature as closely as possible. Continue to stir and slowly add the lemon juice. Leave the mixture to set for 15 minutes. If no curds form, simply add more lemon juice.

2. Line a colander with muslin and ladle in the curds to settle and cool for 30 minutes. Gather the muslin by the corners and hang it for as long as necessary to remove the whey.

3. Salt to 1% by weight, break up the curds so that more whey comes out, then pack into muslin-lined moulds, wrap up and store in the fridge until ready to use.

Queso Fresco

This is similar to queso blanco, but made with rennet.

2.5 litres each buttermilk and full-fat milk
5 drops rennet, mixed in 1–2 tablespoons cooled, boiled water
Salt

1. Pour both milks into a large pan and allow to attain room temperature. Using a bain marie, slowly heat to 34°C. Once it has attained this temperature, add the rennet and mix well. Leave for 60 minutes to set, then cut the curd into 2cm cubes.

2. Raise the temperature to 40°C and leave the curds for 15 minutes to cook. Drain them into a colander lined with cheesecloth. Twist the cheesecloth so that the curds form a ball and squeeze out the whey.

3. Open the cloth and break the curds, then add 1% salt by weight: this will bring out more whey. Roll the cheese into a ball and store in the fridge until ready to use.

Mascarpone

This simple cream cheese will save you a fortune if you make your own. It is the best cheese you can use for making tiramisu or cheesecake.

1 litre double cream
2g (¼ teaspoon) tartaric acid

1. In a pan, slowly and carefully heat the cream to 80°C. Do not let it catch or you will alter the flavour. This is best done by using a double boiler or bain marie.

2. Add the tartaric acid and stir for 10 minutes; very fine curds should form. If not, add a pinch more (0.5g) and stir for another 10 minutes. Keep on stirring carefully, without too much vigour.

3. With a double (or even triple) layer of fine, dampened cheesecloth in a colander, carefully strain off the whey.

4. Leave it for 90 minutes to strain, then put the colander into the fridge overnight in a bowl to collect the drips.

5. The cheese is now ready and can be sweetened or eaten as required.

SWEET CHEESE DISHES

Kova

Kova is an Indian sweet made of buttered, sweetened cheese. It is very sweet indeed and can be served alone or with ice cream.

75g butter
225g soft cheese
225g powdered milk
225g sugar

1. Gently heat the butter until it has melted. Add all the other ingredients.

2. Put the pan over a low heat and stir until the mixture attains a golden brown colour.

3. Cool to room temperature and serve.

Simple Cheesecake

This is the simplest cheesecake you can make. This one is flavoured with lemon, but try it with a lime or an orange instead. It is delicious served with fruit or a chocolate sauce.

SERVES 6

250g digestive biscuits
100g butter
300g soft cheese (any type will do)
180g icing sugar juice and zest of 1 lemon
300ml whipping cream

1. Butter a loose-bottomed 22cm round cake tin.

2. Put the digestive biscuits into a plastic food bag and use a rolling pin to bash them to crumbs.

3. Melt the butter gently in a pan and stir in the biscuit crumbs. Press the mixture down firmly into the bottom of the tin and chill for about 45 minutes.

4. Meanwhile, make the filling. Cream the cheese, icing sugar, lemon juice and zest together in a bowl.

5. In a separate bowl, whip the cream until it forms soft peaks, but is not stiff. Fold this into the cheese mixture.

6. Spread evenly over the chilled base and return to the fridge. Leave to firm up for 1½ hours before serving.

Tiramisu

This traditional Italian dessert is very easy to make and is a great favourite in our family.

SERVES 6

100ml single cream
3 egg yolks
500g mascarpone cheese
3 rounded tablespoons caster sugar
350ml very strong coffee
50–80ml brandy
20–22 ratafia or sponge fingers
1 heaped tablespoon cocoa

1. Beat the cream and egg yolks into the mascarpone cheese.

2. Beat in the sugar.

3. In another bowl, combine the coffee and brandy. Dip the sponge fingers into the mixture and lay them close together in a deep rectangular dish. When they have covered the base, spread a layer of the cheese mixture evenly over them. Repeat this until all the biscuits and cream have been used up.

4. Sieve the cocoa over the top very generously.

5. Chill for 1½ hours before serving.

Vanilla Ice Cream

This ice cream uses ricotta in its ingredients, and it gives a tang to the finished ice cream which still remains very creamy.

4 whole eggs
2 egg yolks
150g caster sugar
300ml double cream
200g ricotta
120ml full-fat milk
1 teaspoon vanilla extract

1. Whisk the eggs, yolks and sugar together in a bowl.

2. In a saucepan, heat the cream, ricotta, milk and vanilla together, whisking gently. When the cream is hot, remove it from the heat and stir it into the egg mixture, then pour the custard back into the pan.

3. Return to the heat, whisking gently as the custard thickens. Cool for 10 minutes.

4. Pour into a freezable container and, when cold, freeze for 1 hour. Then remove and beat with a wooden spoon.

5. Repeat the beating after the second hour, then leave to freeze completely for about 4 hours.

6. When you are ready to serve the ice cream, remove it from the freezer 10 minutes before serving, unless the weather is very warm. This will help enable you to serve it more easily.

COMMON CHEESE-MAKING PROBLEMS

Many problems can crop up when cheese-making; at times it seems as if everything is against you and the problems mount up. The best response is not to be afraid and press on: if you stick to temperatures and techniques, all will work out well.

I confess that I've probably made every possible mistake. There have been curds too fine to collect; funny flavours; difficult setting cheeses; presses falling over; cheeses breaking up; lots of moulds spoiling the cheese; too much salt; too little salt – and this is only a small part of a very long list. So why make cheese at all? After all, you can buy the 'real thing' for very little money and not have the problems of trying to make the stuff. All I can say is that some of us are driven to master things, and food is probably the most important occupation to master. Without the ability to make these products at home, we are left at the mercy of shops and supermarkets.

Nothing is perfect

One thing to bear in mind when using this book is that you will never replicate these recipes, which are themselves imperfect, perfectly or exactly. Conditions in your kitchen are different from mine, and you will have to adapt what you are doing in order to make cheese. Right from the start you will be making decisions about what is and isn't right, changing recipes and adding your own touch. This is perfectly normal, but there will be problems along the way. Please consider this book as the beginning of your cheese-making life and keep at it. You will find your way of cheese-making because no two people will ever do it in quite the same way.

Avoiding contamination

There is a real problem with using books about cheese-making when it comes to instructions regarding cleanliness. The majority of books are written with the dairy in mind: a place where nothing else happens except the production of cheese, butter and cream. However, this book is about cheese-making in the home, and there can be many potential contamination problems associated with working in a domestic kitchen.

Particularly when it comes to maturing cheese, you must be certain that there is no chance of contamination. Taints are bad enough; it is amazing how cheese absorbs flavours in the air, and if you're making a lot of curries, or like garlic and onions, your cheeses will pick up the flavour if you're not careful.

Microbes and maturation

Another potential problem area concerns the cleanliness of your kitchen itself. It isn't – despite all the cleaners, disinfectants and bleaches – a microbe-free environment. This has an impact on both the flavour and safety of homemade cheese, which is why it's imperative that cheese is matured in clean conditions.

Also be aware that you are making small cheeses, not huge factory ones. This has a number of implications. Firstly, there is comparatively a larger surface area to volume when making small cheeses. They also dry out more quickly, and there is a greater chance of them failing. For these reasons, it is best to mature your cheese inside sterile plastic containers; just be sure to remove the lid from time to time in order to change the air inside.

You can, of course, stand cheese on cheese mats inside the boxes, but make sure the cheese cannot be contaminated by fingers, sneezes, other foods, etc.

Odd, sharp or bitter flavours

The most common reason for bitterness or oddness in cheese is contamination. Microbes from non-sterilised equipment, spoiled milk, bad maturation conditions and poor personal hygiene can all spoil cheese. I'm sorry to repeat this mantra yet again, but you have to be really clean when making cheese. Cleanliness is the most important part of home cheese-making.

Other possible areas for microbe growth include not adding enough salt. I have purposely reduced the amount of salt added to the cheese recipes in this book, but there is still enough present to cut down the microbes in the cheese. Don't skimp on the salt; there are few recipes that do not add salt, and those that do must be eaten straight away.

Similarly, leaving cheese to ripen too long at the beginning of the cheese-making process might introduce too much acid into the mix. Stick to the timings given in the recipes, and if you do happen to leave the milk to ripen for too long, just add a little more milk to dilute it, or else cool it a little before using.

Problems with starters

There are a number of reasons why starters can go wrong. Firstly (and increasingly in these days of factory-farming), the milk you use can contain antibiotics which kill bacteria. If the starter doesn't really change the milk at all, then the starter itself might be old or killed by too much heat.

Sometimes your starter gives off gas, and you get fizzy or bubbly milk. This is caused by a lack of cleanliness and the introduction of unwanted microbes; the batch should, sadly, be discarded.

Rennet

Adding too much rennet is also a common cause of bad flavours in cheese-making. My first cheese was spoiled because I simply didn't understand the important rule of adding only a small amount of rennet: too much, and the cheese will develop a very odd flavour. I must have added 25 drops to 4.5 litres of milk in my first batch and this made the cheese taste really harsh.

Blandness

The problem of blandness is one that has a few causes. Frequently it is simply because not enough salt has been added to the cheese. The recipes I use generally don't insist on a lot of salt, but really, saltiness is a matter of personal taste. So whenever the instructions say 'Add 1% salt by weight', you can instead just salt until you like it.

Remember, too, that a cheese's flavour changes over time, and the maturation process is important. You might simply have tried your cheese too early, which is a great temptation.

A final problem is caused when you either forget or don't add enough starter, which then does not have enough acidity, and the texture and flavour of the cheese both suffer. A lack of creaminess in cheese is also due to a lack of starter.

Tiny curds

Sometimes you get curds that can't be saved by cheesecloth. There are a number of reasons for this. Milk that is too hot makes cheese coagulate in flecks, but usually small curds are due to too much acidity. Stick to the timings in the recipes and you should be able to avoid this problem.

Generally speaking, it takes about ten minutes for rennet to work, so if it blasts away right from the start, then the curds are likely to be very tiny and not set into a solid mass. I generally try to let curds settle, often by standing them on a stone floor where there are few vibrations, and then trying to catch them in three layers of damp muslin. You can ladle as much of the whey off as possible before trying to catch the flecks. Another technique is to bring small curds to the boil, making what might be described as an 'emergency ricotta'.

Lack of set

This is probably the most soul-destroying part of cheese-making. You set up, do everything you are told – and nothing happens. You add a little more rennet, and still nothing! A lack of set is usually down to ineffective rennet, so check the use-by date on the packet and buy new if you have to. To keep it at its most effective, always keep rennet out of the sunlight and store it in the fridge.

You can also hamper rennet by overheating it. Because it is an enzyme, rennet is a very complex molecule which can be destroyed by too much heat. On the whole, proteins degrade at temperatures above 40°C, so be sure to add rennet only to cool water.

Another reason for a lack of set is trying to make cheese with cold milk. Rennet really doesn't work at temperatures lower than 25°C, which is really low in itself. Most cheeses are made at temperatures of around 28°C to 30°C.

Different forms of spoilage

Spoilage is most obvious wherever you see mould growing on the surface of your cheese. You want this to happen with some cheeses, but in those cases you've inoculated the cheese with a specific bacterium or fungus in the first place. If an unwanted mould is blue, you can mostly remove it, but this really isn't the best option. I would advise discarding a cheese that shows any kind of unexpected mould growth. This kind of spoilage can arise from a maturation temperature that is too warm, or from very high humidity, so cool down and blow the moisture away.

The second form of spoilage occurs when you cannot get a cheese out of its mould. This is because microbes in the milk, or any that have been introduced during the cheese-making process, have given off gas, which then expands the cheese in the mould. Any 'stuck' cheeses should thus be discarded.

Similarly, if you get unexpected holes in a cheese – usually small ones – then the same type of bacteria are in action, and you should discard this cheese, too.

Another frequent problem in this kind of spoilage is an insufficiently sterilised cheesecloth. You should not expect a new cloth to be sterile; it should be boiled before use. Bacteria on the surface of the cloth glues it to the cheese, and again, should this happen, you should discard the cheese.

Remember, cheesecloth or muslin is an organic material. If you were to look at it under the microscope you would find a lot of fibres, which have a collected surface area measured in tens of metres: plenty of room for bacteria to hide.

Moisture appearing on the cheese

When cheese matures, whey or moisture appears on the surface or at the base; this is a sign that the cheese hasn't been drained enough. It might be that you haven't pressed it enough or turned it, which allows whey to pool around it. Usually this whey spoils cheese because it is comparatively high in sugar.

To avoid this problem, make sure you turn the cheese over daily when maturing. This will allow evaporation to take place from all surfaces rather than having the top dry out and the bottom remain relatively wet.

You can also get this problem if using buttermilk or yoghurt as a starter, so be especially careful when making cheeses that call for them in a recipe.

INDEX

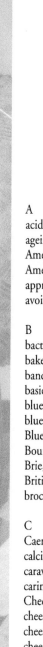

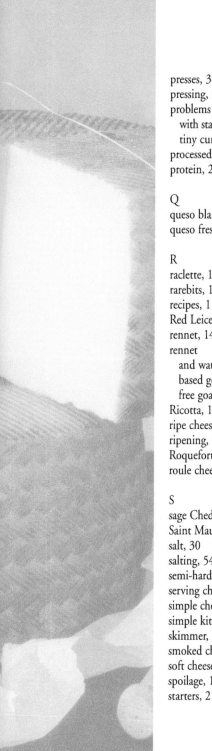